# Library
# Research Guide
# to
# Music

# "Library Research Guides" Series

JAMES R. KENNEDY, JR. and
THOMAS G. KIRK, JR., Editors

# Library Research Guide to Music

## Illustrated Search Strategy and Sources

by
JOHN E. DRUESEDOW, JR.
Music Librarian
Oberlin College

("Library Research Guides" Series, No. 6)

Pierian Press
ANN ARBOR, MICHIGAN

International Standard Book Numbers:  0-87650-138-2  (cloth)
                                      0-87650-139-0  (paper)
Library of Congress Catalog Card Number:  LC 81-86634

Pierian Press, P.O. Box 1808, Ann Arbor, Michigan  48106
Printed in the United States of America

Note: Double hyphens have been used throughout the text
in place of dashes to indicate inclusive numberings.

# Contents

# Preface

This book has been written primarily for the undergraduate music student who is preparing to write on the subject of music, perhaps for the first time. It is a guide for the gathering and winnowing — the selection and evaluation — of source materials for medium-length term papers. Similar to other texts in the Library Research Guides Series published by Pierian Press, it takes the form of a "case study." A hypothetical topic is proposed and developed with reference to major research resources and is carried through to the point where the student would begin to do the actual preliminary writing.

Although research at the undergraduate level is emphasized here, the graduate student may find the discussions of reference works helpful in preparing to write a thesis or in reviewing for a music bibliography examination. Those who teach college music may also be able to use this guide, as a text or as a source for supplementary readings for a variety of courses which require library research.

Before launching into a term paper with the aid of this guide, one should have some familiarity with the library card catalog and a basic periodical index such as the *Readers' Guide to Periodical Literature*. Anyone who has gained competence with these tools will probably be able to deal with most of the materials presented here with little difficulty. Those who are not sure they can cope with the card catalog or the *Readers' Guide* are strongly urged to complete the quiz in Appendix I. It can then be determined if further background is needed, and, if so, one should consult a manual such as Margaret G. Cook's *The New Library Key*, 3d ed. (New York: H.W. Wilson, 1975).

Not covered in this guide are the typographical mechanics of writing papers, including the construction of headings, footnotes, illustrative examples, the format of bibliographies, and so forth. Readers who are interested in these aspects of writing should consider such texts as Kate L. Turabian's *A Manual for Writers of Term Papers, Theses, and Dissertations*, 4th ed. (Chicago: University of Chicago, 1973), or the *MLA Handbook for Writers of Research Papers, Theses, and Dissertations* (New York: Modern Language Association, 1977). Style manuals designed especially for music research include the following: Eugene Helm and Albert T. Luper, *Words and Music* (Hackensack, NJ: Joseph Boonin, 1971), and Demar B. Irvine, *Writing about Music*, 2d ed. (Seattle: University of Washington, 1968). Any of these texts may be used in conjunction with this guide.

There have been comparatively few books written in English on the subject of music research, and most of them have been directed to the graduate student. Ruth T. Watanabe's *Introduction to Music Research* (Englewood Cliffs, NJ: Prentice-Hall, 1967) has remained the standard text on the subject for more than a decade; it deserves to be read by all students of music, especially those at the graduate level. The present guide, while not intended to supplant the Watanabe text, attempts to deal with the problems of the undergraduate in a special way by examining a particular topic from the "moment of discovery," through various stages of refinement, to final acceptance and somewhat beyond. This approach is based on the double premise that, for the undergraduate especially, the selection and refinement of a topic are important aspects of research and that the "learn by doing" method can be fruitful in the field of bibliography.

# Acknowledgments

It would have been impossible to complete this book without the patient guidance and diligent editorial care provided by James R. Kennedy, Jr., who has himself written other books in the Pierian Press Library Research Guides Series. I am immensely grateful for his help. My gratitude is also extended to a number of members of the Oberlin College Library staff, who have expressed interest and encouragement. And I deeply appreciate the generous support and valuable advice offered by members of my family, especially my wife Elaine.

Permission from publishers to use excerpts from reference books and other published materials under copyright was in most cases speedily and cheerfully granted; the fine spirit of cooperation shown by all those listed below has been gratifying. In some cases, a special wording of the permission statement has been requested, and this wording appears in the captions for the illustrative figures. The following is a complete list of figures and includes citations for some materials which are not copyrighted.

Figure 1: Apel, Willi. *Harvard Dictionary of Music*. 2d ed., rev. and enl. Cambridge, MA: Belknap Press of Harvard University Press, 1969, pp. 403, 404, 331.

Figure 2: Thompson, Oscar, ed. *The International Cyclopedia of Music and Musicians*. 10th ed., edited by Bruce Bohle. New York: Dodd, Mead, 1975, pp. 527, 536.

Figure 3: *Baker's Biographical Dictionary of Musicians*. 6th ed., completely rev. by Nicolas Slonimsky. New York: Schirmer Books, 1978, p. 390.

Figure 4: *The New Grove Dictionary of Music and Musicians*. Edited by Stanley Sadie. London: Macmillan, 1980, vol. 5, pp. 313, xii.

Figure 5: *Die Musik in Geschichte und Gegenwart. Allgemeine Enzyklopädie der Musik*. Edited by Friedrich Blume. Kassel und Basel: Bärenreiter, 1949–69, vol. 3, p. v, col. 75.

Figure 6: *Riemann Musik Lexikon*. 12th ed., edited by Wilibald Gurlitt. Mainz: B. Schott's Söhne, 1959–74; Ergänzungsband: Personenteil, L-Z, p. 727; Ergänzungsband: Personenteil, A-K, pp. ix,xii.

Figure 7: *Encyclopédie de la musique*. Publié sous la direction de François Lesure et Vladimir Féderov. Paris: Fasquelle, 1958–61, vol. 1, p. 641.

Figure 8: Abravanel, Claude. *Claude Debussy: A Bibliography*. Detroit: Information Coordinators, 1974, pp. 70, 74.

Figure 9: Catalog cards.

Figure 10: *Library of Congress Subject Headings*. 9th ed. Washington, DC: Library of Congress, 1980, vol. 2, pp. 1552, 1550, 1551.

Figure 11: Catalog cards.

Figure 12: Catalog card.

Figure 13: Catalog card.

Figure 14: Lockspeiser, Edward. *Debussy: His Life and Mind*. New York: Macmillan, 1962, vol. 2, pp. vii, 335.

Figure 15: *The Music Index. 1963 Annual Cumulation*. Detroit: Information Coordinators, p. 218, p. from list of abbreviations.

Figure 16: Krohn, Ernst C., comp. *The History of Music: An Index to the Literature Available in a Selected Group of Musicological Publications*. St. Louis: Baton Music Co., 1958, p. 340.

Figure 17: *The New York Times Index, 1978: A Book of Record*. New York: New York Times, 1979, pp. 975, 681.

Figure 18: Duckles, Vincent. *Music Reference and Research Materials: An Annotated Bibliography*. 3d ed. New York: The Free Press, 1974. pp. 471, 335.

Figure 19: Bobillier, Marie (Michel Brenet, pseud.). "Bibliographie des bibliographies musicales." In *L'Année musicale*, 3 (1913), 1–152. Reprint, New York: Da Capo, 1971, pp. 71, 51.

Figure 20: *RILM Abstracts of Music Literature*. Edited by Barry S. Brook. New York: International RILM Center, 1967– . *Cumulative Index I–V (1967-1971)*, pp. 69, 264; vol. 4, no. 1 (Jan.-April, 1970), pp. 53, 105, 107.

Figure 21: *Bibliographie des Musikschrifttums. 1967*. Leipzig, Frankfurt am Main: Hofmeister, pp. 148, 149.

Figure 22: *The Music Index. 1967 Annual Cumulation*. Detroit: Information Coordinators, p. 288.

Figure 23: Sears, Minnie Earl. *Song Index: An Index to More Than 12000 Songs in 177 Song Collections Comprising 262 Volumes*. New York: H. W. Wilson, 1926, pp. 536, 101, xxxi.

"B.C." comic strips. By permission of John Hart and Field Newspaper Syndicate.

# Introduction

"To achieve good and accurate writing about music is as rare an accomplishment as expert wine-tasting . . ."
— Nat Shapiro (from *An Encyclopedia of Quotations about Music*).

## The Uncertainties of the Uninitiated

It is the rare music student indeed who rejoices at the announcement of a written assignment or term paper. (Music students are no different from other students in this regard.) If you are one who feels the pangs of uncertainty at the thought of wandering through a forest of library shelves, who becomes bewildered in attempts to decipher cryptic abbreviations in indexes and bibliographies, or who suffers remorse for having "left something out" of the final draft of your paper, then perhaps this guide will ease your burden.

## Writing and the Pitfalls of Disorganization

For most persons, writing that is clear, concise, fluent, and accurate is not easy, to say the least. Careful writers learn quickly that writing is very time-consuming. Much thought and planning are required in the search for the correct word, the most pertinent reference, or the best overall framework. Polishing each successive draft calls for patience and persistence.

Writing usually requires several stages of development, and organization is required at each stage. If you have ever approached the reference shelves or the card catalog in your library without really knowing where to begin — or have started out with the notion that there are one or two books which contain all the information you need for your paper — then the chances are very good that your writing will be disorganized. You will have jeopardized your paper at the research stage.

## Search Strategy

This is where "search strategy," or research methodology, comes in. You will discover, with the aid of this guide, that there can be a systematic method of finding an appropriate topic and of locating the information you need from the most important library sources. You will find that your general methodology, as well as the sources you consult, can make a difference in the degree of success you achieve in writing your paper. At the very least, a good search strategy will improve your efficiency in the information gathering process and may lead you toward a topic that is compatible with your interests, background, and research experience.

## Research

The word "research" is sometimes associated only with the scientific disciplines. There is no question that experimentation in a chemistry laboratory, for example, may properly be referred to as research. It is also appropriate to include the scholarly activity of gathering, assimilating, and reporting information of a humanistic nature in the research category. In fact, in the most general sense, almost any information seeking activity can be called research.

## The Benefits of Labor

When you have finished your term paper — when the last typographical error is corrected, the last bibliographical citation checked, the last example inserted, all punctuated with a heavy sigh of relief — you should expect to realize the benefits of your labors. In a general sense, you will have refined your skills in thinking, organizing, and writing. And these newly refined skills will not necessarily be limited to scholarly endeavors: it is possible that your overall ability to communicate will be enhanced. Furthermore, it is quite likely that you will *know* the material in your paper far better than facts and figures learned for an examination. As in the case of a meticulously rehearsed piece of music, your writing will have become part of your "repertoire" of knowledge.

"Let music sound while he
doth make his choice . . . "
— Shakespeare (from *The
Merchant of Venice*).

## Topics: Assigned and Unassigned

If you have read the Introduction to this guide, you should be convinced that good writing is difficult but rewarding. Choosing a topic — the beginning of the writing process — may be inferred to be difficult also, but not without rewards. But what about the assigned topic, which automatically eliminates this difficulty? Such topics are, after all, somewhat commonplace, especially at the undergraduate level.

Actually, the assigned topic, one that you would not necessarily have chosen yourself, may prove to be a somewhat mixed blessing. Unless it sparks and sustains your enthusiasm and powers of concentration, the final product — your term paper — may not be representative of your best efforts. Therefore, if you have the opportunity to choose, do so, keeping in mind that it is helpful to deal with a topic about which you have some knowledge already, some background to build upon.

## The "Case Study" Approach

Let us imagine, for the sake of building a "case study," that you are taking a course in twentieth-century music and are especially interested in the movement known as Impressionism. Your first task is to find out more about this movement in order to determine its suitability as a topic.

Why not plunge right in and begin drafting an outline as soon as a few books and articles are collected? One reason should be persuasive: at this stage, you have not yet established that "Impressionism" is a tailor-made topic for you, nor have you surveyed the range of library sources available to you. Choosing a topic does not necessarily mean selecting the first idea that comes to mind.

Very often, students who have had little writing experience fix upon subject matter that is entirely too broad to be covered adequately in a term paper of about twenty to thirty pages. If, for example, whole books have been written on a particular topic, then chances are extremely good that a term paper on the same topic would provide only a summary, or at worst only a hodge-podge of loosely connected sections.

One objective in writing a term paper is to achieve some degree of originality or to be creative in presenting the insights *you* have had in studying and assimilating the information you have collected. This objective can be met only with great difficulty if your topic is too broad.

It follows that if your topic is chosen with great care, the materials supporting your research on this topic should be selected with discrimination. If you do not make a thorough survey of the available library materials, you will have no assurance that you are drawing upon those which are most authoritative and appropriate.

## Surveying the Field of Dictionaries and Encyclopedias

Let us go on to investigate the topic "Impressionism" a bit. Even if you are quite familiar with examples of music labeled impressionistic, you should consult an authoritative dictionary or encyclopedia to find out more about the movement itself, its rise and decline, geographical centers of activity, chief representatives, and so forth. The very important first step in your search for information is to find articles which summarize.

A good place to begin is the *Harvard Dictionary of Music*, by Willi Apel, 2d ed. (Cambridge, MA: The Belknap Press of Harvard University Press, 1969), considered one of the most important music reference works in English (especially among one-volume publications). It is important to note that the *Harvard Dictionary* does not contain strictly biographical articles, although many names are mentioned. As FIGURE 1 shows, the article on impressionism (pp. 403-404) is replete with names. This article also contains several cross-references (marked with an asterisk or square brackets) to other articles in the dictionary, plus a brief bibliography of books and articles.

## Measuring the Breadth of Your Topic

Can we determine from this article if "Impressionism" as a topic for a term paper is too broad? Before answering this question, let us examine some of the criteria for measuring the breadth of a topic:

1.  Historical, chronological limits.
2.  Geographical limits.
3.  Biographical limits.

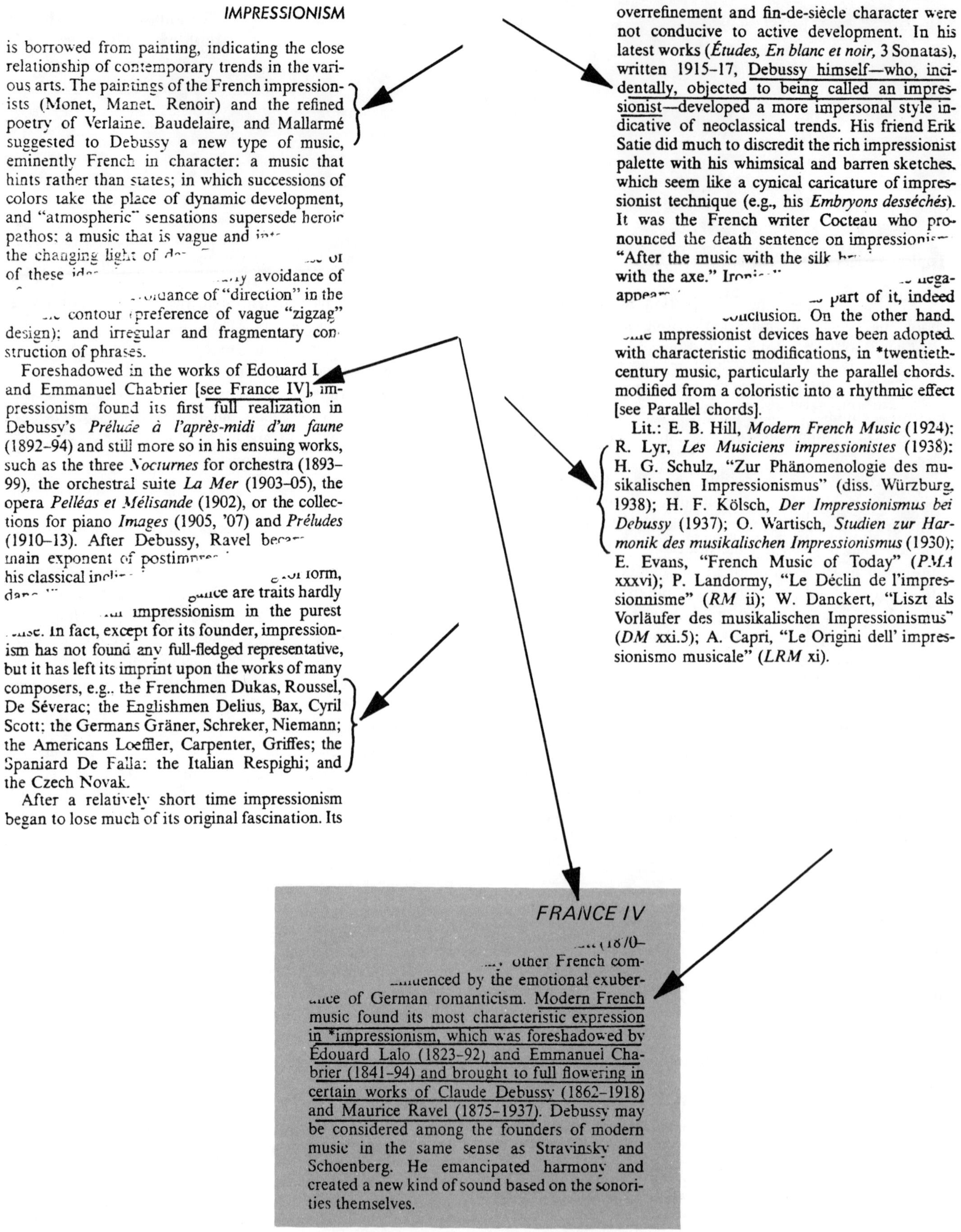

is borrowed from painting, indicating the close relationship of contemporary trends in the various arts. The paintings of the French impressionists (Monet, Manet, Renoir) and the refined poetry of Verlaine, Baudelaire, and Mallarmé suggested to Debussy a new type of music, eminently French in character: a music that hints rather than states; in which successions of colors take the place of dynamic development, and "atmospheric" sensations supersede heroic pathos; a music that is vague and int~~
the changing light of d~~ ~~ ~~ of
of these ide~~ ~~ ~~y avoidance of
~~ ~~ ~~oidance of "direction" in the
~~ ~~ contour (preference of vague "zigzag" design); and irregular and fragmentary construction of phrases.

Foreshadowed in the works of Edouard L~~ and Emmanuel Chabrier [see France IV], impressionism found its first full realization in Debussy's *Prélude à l'après-midi d'un faune* (1892–94) and still more so in his ensuing works, such as the three *Nocturnes* for orchestra (1893–99), the orchestral suite *La Mer* (1903–05), the opera *Pelléas et Mélisande* (1902), or the collections for piano *Images* (1905, '07) and *Préludes* (1910–13). After Debussy, Ravel bec~~
main exponent of postimpr~~
his classical incli~~ ~~ ~~ ~~ ~~ ~~or form,
dan~~ ~~ ~~ ~~ ~~ ~~ance are traits hardly
~~ ~~ impressionism in the purest
~~ ~~se. In fact, except for its founder, impressionism has not found any full-fledged representative, but it has left its imprint upon the works of many composers, e.g., the Frenchmen Dukas, Roussel, De Séverac; the Englishmen Delius, Bax, Cyril Scott; the Germans Gräner, Schreker, Niemann; the Americans Loeffler, Carpenter, Griffes; the Spaniard De Falla; the Italian Respighi; and the Czech Novak.

After a relatively short time impressionism began to lose much of its original fascination. Its overrefinement and fin-de-siècle character were not conducive to active development. In his latest works (*Études, En blanc et noir,* 3 Sonatas), written 1915–17, Debussy himself—who, incidentally, objected to being called an impressionist—developed a more impersonal style indicative of neoclassical trends. His friend Erik Satie did much to discredit the rich impressionist palette with his whimsical and barren sketches, which seem like a cynical caricature of impressionist technique (e.g., his *Embryons desséchés*). It was the French writer Cocteau who pronounced the death sentence on impressioni~~
"After the music with the silk b~~
with the axe." Ironic~~ ~~ ~~ ~~ ~~ ~~ega-
appea~~ ~~ ~~ ~~ ~~ part of it, indeed
~~ ~~ ~~nclusion. On the other hand,
~~ ~~e impressionist devices have been adopted, with characteristic modifications, in *twentieth-century music, particularly the parallel chords, modified from a coloristic into a rhythmic effect [see Parallel chords].

Lit.: E. B. Hill, *Modern French Music* (1924); R. Lyr, *Les Musiciens impressionistes* (1938); H. G. Schulz, "Zur Phänomenologie des musikalischen Impressionismus" (diss. Würzburg, 1938); H. F. Kölsch, *Der Impressionismus bei Debussy* (1937); O. Wartisch, *Studien zur Harmonik des musikalischen Impressionismus* (1930); E. Evans, "French Music of Today" (*PMA* xxxvi); P. Landormy, "Le Déclin de l'impressionnisme" (*RM* ii); W. Danckert, "Liszt als Vorläufer des musikalischen Impressionismus" (*DM* xxi.5); A. Capri, "Le Origini dell' impressionismo musicale" (*LRM* xi).

FRANCE IV

~~ ~~ (1870–
~~ ~~ other French com-
~~ ~~uenced by the emotional exuber-
~~ ~~nce of German romanticism. Modern French music found its most characteristic expression in *impressionism, which was foreshadowed by Édouard Lalo (1823–92) and Emmanuel Chabrier (1841–94) and brought to full flowering in certain works of Claude Debussy (1862–1918) and Maurice Ravel (1875–1937). Debussy may be considered among the founders of modern music in the same sense as Stravinsky and Schoenberg. He emancipated harmony and created a new kind of sound based on the sonorities themselves.

Figure 1. Harvard Dictionary of Music.

4. Interdisciplinary aspects.

5. Source materials available.

These criteria can be applied to the information in the *Harvard Dictionary* as follows:

1. In following up the cross-reference "[see France IV]" on page 403, we find on page 331 a statement which sets out the general chronological limits for the topic: "Modern French music found its most characteristic expression in impressionism, which was foreshadowed by Édouard Lalo (1823–92) and Emmanuel Chabrier (1841–94) and brought to full flowering in certain works of Claude Debussy (1862–1918) and Maurice Ravel (1875–1937)." It is possible to infer from this statement that we are speaking of the period roughly from 1870 or 1880 to about 1920 or 1930 – a time span of up to sixty years, approximately.

2. On page 403 again, we see that the French movement influenced composers from England, Germany, the United States, Spain, Italy, and Czechoslovakia. It is clear that the movement was widespread geographically.

3. It is also clear that the topic encompasses the life and works of more than a dozen composers, some prolific and well-known.

4. If the topic were to be covered adequately, the French impressionistic movement in painting would merit passing reference; the French poetry of the same period would also deserve consideration.

5. In the bibliography on page 404, several books on impressionism are mentioned. This suggests that the topic does require extended treatment.

Thus, in the light of two articles from an authoritative dictionary, the topic "Impressionism," or "Musical Impressionism" if you wish to express it more precisely, appears to be of considerable breadth. It would probably overrun the boundaries of the average term paper.

Important questions arise: Has the search led into a blind alley? Is it necessary to start over?

In many cases, you will not have to "start from scratch" again. A good search strategy allows for refinement and modification of the original topic, not abandonment. In this case, you have made contact with a major reference tool and have learned to interpret it in order to determine that your first choice for a topic needs further consideration. This can be considered progress.

## Taking Notes

Before going on, you should prepare a note card, with annotations, on the articles you have examined. The bibliographic citation – the heading you wish to use for your note card – should take the form you intend to use in your paper. Therefore, you should have the style manual you have chosen close by so that you can refer to it whenever necessary. By following this procedure religiously after the examination of each important piece of material, you will ultimately save time and avoid much frustration.

## Pressing On

Your interest in impressionism persists. The *Harvard Dictionary* article has called to your attention an interesting point: the major representative of the movement, Claude Debussy, "objected to being called an impressionist" (p. 404). Now why should this be so? This question remains intriguing, but unanswered, as you continue to consult dictionary and encyclopedia articles for ideas to impart a new direction to your search.

The article on impressionism in *The International Cyclopedia of Music and Musicians*, 10th ed., edited by Bruce Bohle (New York: Dodd, Mead, 1975), is somewhat more detailed than the one in the *Harvard Dictionary* and gives a longer list of representative composers (see pp. 1062–1063). Immediately following is an article on impressionistic methods (pp. 1063–1064), which provides a catalog of technical devices found in various impressionistic compositions. It is important to note that neither of these articles has a bibliography. This omission is characteristic of *The International Cyclopedia* (sometimes called Thompson's, after Oscar Thompson, a distinguished lexicographer and the first editor of this publication) and limits the work's usefulness for your present purposes. At this stage of the game, you need bibliographical references to continue the thread of your investigation. On the plus side is the fact that these articles are signed (both by Marion Bauer), indicating (usually) a noteworthy degree of authority in a multi-author publication such as an encyclopedia or dictionary. You will recall that one of your objectives is not only to find material, but to find material having the hallmarks of authority and reliability.

## An Important Turning Point

As the question about Debussy nags at the back of your mind, you decide that *some aspect* of the life and works of this renowned French composer might prove fruitful for your research. If you are a performer, perhaps you have worked on the *Préludes* (Books I and II, 1910–13), for piano, or the *Chansons de Bilitis* (*Songs of Bilitis*, 1897–1898), for voice. As a listener you may have found a special enjoyment in the orchestral tone poems, such as *Prélude à l'après midi d'un faune* (*Prelude to the Afternoon of a Faun*, 1892–94) or *La Mer* (*The Sea*, 1903–05). Perhaps you have been privileged to attend a production of the opera, *Pelléas et Mélisande* (*Pelléas and Mélisande*), first produced in 1902. Your interest in Debussy grows as you contemplate the possibilities.

*The International Cyclopedia* just happens to be rather strong in biography. The article on Debussy is excerpted in FIGURE 2. By Oscar Thompson himself, it gives a detailed account of the life and works (pp. 527–535), a "Calendar of Debussy's Life" (pp. 535–536), and a catalog of musical compositions (arranged by genre and date) and literary works

# CLAUDE DEBUSSY

(b. Saint-Germain-en-Laye, Aug. 22, 1862—d. Paris, March 25, 1918)

## ⟶ BY *Oscar Thompson*

### I. LIFE

ACHILLE-CLAUDE DEBUSSY (he dropped the Achille when he came to maturity) was born in Saint-Germain-en-Laye, within sight of Paris, on Aug. 22, 1862. The man who was to sign himself "musicien français" and whom Gabriel d'Annunzio was to dub "Claude de France" came of a line of farm labourers, city artisans and small merchants. Though in his later 'teens he wrote his name De Bussy, this was only the caprice of a youth who may have sought to give the impression that he was of noble blood. A distant ancestor, it is true, was born in a town only about five miles distant from Bussy-le-Grand, where the Counts de Buss⟨...⟩ their seat; but nothing other than romantic⟨...⟩ can link Debussy's family with that w⟨...⟩ best known representative Roger⟨...⟩ known as Bussy-Rabutin, w⟨...⟩ esque libertine of the la⟨...⟩ father, Manuel-Ach⟨...⟩ phie Manoury ⟨...⟩ there—38 ⟨...⟩

Ach⟨...⟩

2⟨...⟩

protégé. Mme. Roustan played a considerable part ⟨'⟩ bringing up the Debussy children, though it w⟨...⟩ that the mother devoted herself to Claud⟨...⟩ shy, sweet, stubborn and "different⟨...⟩ bussy planned a life as a sailor ⟨...⟩ than an admiral!) for his so⟨n...⟩ sending him to a nautic⟨...⟩ Mme. Roustan) ta⟨...⟩ ucation—he se⟨...⟩ ⟨...⟩mer-⟨...⟩ piece, later year⟨...⟩ ⟨...⟩ie conducts his a⟨...⟩ Rome. He re-

⟨...⟩or cancer. Writes two ⟨...⟩n dies.)
⟨...⟩sion of libretto for *La Chute* ⟨...⟩ (Reger dies; Granados drowned ⟨...⟩x, torpedoed by German submarine.) ⟨...⟩es his last work, the Sonata for piano ⟨...⟩ and appears in public for the last time as ⟨...⟩ (May 5) to play the sonata with Gaston ⟨...⟩let. He undergoes a second operation and grows steadily weaker.
⟨...⟩—Debussy dies in Paris (March 25), during long-range bombardment. (Boito, Cui and Parry die.)

### ⟶ CATALOGUE OF DEBUSSY'S WORKS

#### STAGE WORKS

*Pelléas et Mélisande,* opera (1892–1902).
*Rodrigue et Chimène,* opera (unfinished—begun 1890).
*Jeux,* ballet (1912).
*Khamma,* ballet (1912).
*La Boîte à joujoux,* ballet (1913).
*Le Martyre de Saint-Sébastien,* music for D'Annunzio's "Mystery" (1911).

#### ORCHESTRAL WORKS

*Printemps* (1887).
*Prélude à l'Après-midi d'un faune* (1892–94).
*Nocturnes* (1893–99): (1) *Nuages;* (2) *Fêtes;* (3) *Sirènes.*
*La Mer* (1903–05): (1) *De l'aube à midi sur la mer;* (2) *Jeux de vagues;* (3) *Dialogue du vent et de la mer.*
*King Lear,* incidental music (1904): (1) *Fanfare;* (2) *Sommeil de Lear.*
*Images* (1906–12): (1) *Gigues;* (2) *Ibéria;* (3) *Rondes de printemps.*
*Fantaisie,* for solo piano and orchestra (1889).
*Rapsodie,* for saxophone and orchestra (1903–05).
*Danse sacrée* and *Danse profane,* for harp and strings (1904).

**Figure 2. The International Cyclopedia of Music and Musicians.**

---

(pp. 536–538). The format of the catalog is convenient for quick referral to dates and the spelling of titles, something not to be overlooked as you strive for consistency and accuracy in writing your term paper. Again, there is no bibliography.

Bibliographical references are plentiful, however, in *Baker's Biographical Dictionary of Musicians*, 6th ed., edited by Nicolas Slonimsky (New York: Schirmer Books, 1978). If you can adjust to fine print and long paragraphs, *Baker's* can serve you well. For the purpose of obtaining summarizing material — the kind we are looking for now — it complements the *Harvard Dictionary* handily. And in the world of

reference works, where it is not unusual for factual errors to be perpetuated from one work to its derivatives or from one edition to the next, *Baker's*, long under the editorship of Nicolas Slonimsky (who also edited the fifth through the eighth editions of *The International Cyclopedia*), has been especially noted for accuracy. The article on Debussy (pp. 389–391) contains chronological lists of published and unpublished works and a bibliography of books and articles, also arranged chronologically.

## The Large Bibliography

If the Debussy bibliography in the *Baker's* article looks dismayingly large to you, your search strategy is completely "in tune" at this stage. Indeed, it would be impossible to reduce this mountain of material — by rough count over eighty books and articles — to the size of a term paper, even if everything could be obtained in a short period of time. (In all probability, few libraries — even those of major academic institutions — would be able to supply you with all of the items cited here.) If there had been any doubt about the feasibility of such a topic as "Debussy: Life and Works," then that doubt should now be dispelled; it would take a book to do the topic justice.

The question of why Debussy did not wish to be called an "impressionist" is not answered by this article in *Baker's*, even though it is affirmed that "Debussy is regarded as the creator and chief protagonist of musical Impressionism, despite the fact that he deprecated the term and denied his role in the movement." (See p. 390, shown in FIGURE 3.)

---

(1913), and The Hague, Amsterdam, and Rome (1914). Diaghilev produced his ballet, *Jeux*, in Paris, May 15, 1913. Debussy contemplated an American tour with the violinist Arthur Hartmann in 1914, but abandoned the idea because of illness; thereafter his health failed rapidly owing to cancer; and, after two operations, he finally succumbed. Debussy's last appearance in public was on May 5, 1917, when he played (with Gaston Poulet) the piano part of his Violin Sonata. Debussy is regarded as the creator and chief protagonist of musical Impressionism, despite the fact that he deprecated the term and denied his role in the movement. This, however, cannot alter the essential truth that, like Monet in painting and Mallarmé in poetry, Debussy created a style peculiarly sensitive to musical mezzotint from a palette of half-lit delicate

Figure 3. Baker's Biographical Dictionary of Musicians. Permission from Schirmer Books, a division of Macmillan Publishing Co., Inc.

---

## More on the Initial Stage of Research

In this initial stage of your research — the consultation of authoritative summarizing articles in dictionaries and encyclopedias — there is yet another tool to be considered,

and it is an important one: *The New Grove Dictionary of Music and Musicians*, edited by Stanley Sadie (London: Macmillan, 1980; 20 vols.). Preceded by five earlier editions, it is entitled "new" because of very extensive revision and considerable expansion. (The fifth edition is in ten volumes.) Shortly after its publication, it was greeted by glowing reviews and acknowledged as a monument of contemporary musical scholarship. Certainly it cannot be considered as less than *the* standard musical reference work in English, and it is likely to remain so for a generation or more. It is an international dictionary of terms as well as biography. Forms and genres, cities and countries, instruments, ethnic music, organizations and institutions, and a host of other matters are treated, some of them quite extensively. For composers, *The New Grove* has comprehensive lists of works and extensive bibliographies, in chronological order, that can prove to be invaluable.

It is rewarding to peruse the article on Debussy (vol. 5, pp. 292–314), by Roger Nichols. In addition to a detailed biography and a generous amount of analytical commentary on various groups of works, you can find here a number of photographs, musical examples, and facsimiles of pages from original manuscripts. FIGURE 7 (p. 308), for example, is a page from *En blanc et noir* (*In White and Black*), for two pianos. You learn on page 307 that the last movement of this work is dedicated to Stravinsky. Stravinsky?

## A Digression

As this narrative continues, it will become apparent that the last question provides the impetus for further refinement of the topic at hand — we are still considering, at this point, some aspect of Debussy's life and works — and therefore assumes considerable importance in directing the search. It may seem to be a small point: the dedication of one movement of one of Debussy's lesser-known works. Actually, what it most important in this context is the inquiring attitude.

A good researcher is constantly asking questions, some large and some small; some can be answered and others cannot, at least not readily. A finished piece of research, a term paper for example, may contain a few answers and pose a few more questions which remain unsolved. But without the questions, there will be no solutions.

## Dedications

The possible connection between Debussy and Stravinsky arouses your curiosity — the two composers seem worlds apart. Some additional questions occur to you: How important are Debussy's dedications? Were Debussy and Stravinsky acquainted? Are there any stylistic connections between the two? You recall reading in *The International Cyclopedia* that Debussy's ballet *Jeux* (*Play*, 1912) bears some resemblance to Stravinsky's *Le Sacre de printemps* (*The Rite of Spring*, 1911–1913).

Some answers are provided toward the end of the Debussy article in *The New Grove*, in a section entitled, "Debussy and Stravinsky" (p. 310). Here you learn that the two composers met in 1910 and that shortly after the latter's ballet *Petrushka* was brought out, "there followed a period of close friendship, during which Debussy asked Stravinsky's advice about the scoring of *Jeux*, and together they performed the piano-duet version of *The Rite of Spring*, Debussy playing the bass at sight without apparent difficulty." Further on, Stravinsky is reported to have proclaimed that "the musicians of my generation and I myself owe the most to Debussy."

The bibliography lists a journal article on Debussy and Stravinsky in *The Musical Times*. The journal title is abbreviated here, as in the case of many dictionaries, encyclopedias, and indexes, to save space. Abbreviations are usually listed in the front or back of individual volumes, and it is no trouble to look them up if they are not recognizable. FIGURE 4 links the bibliographical citation with the "Bibliographical Abbreviations" section (which begins on p. xi). In the citation, the roman numeral indicates the volume number, and this is followed by the date (1967) and the beginning page number.

**At the Crossroads**

You have now reached an important point of decision:

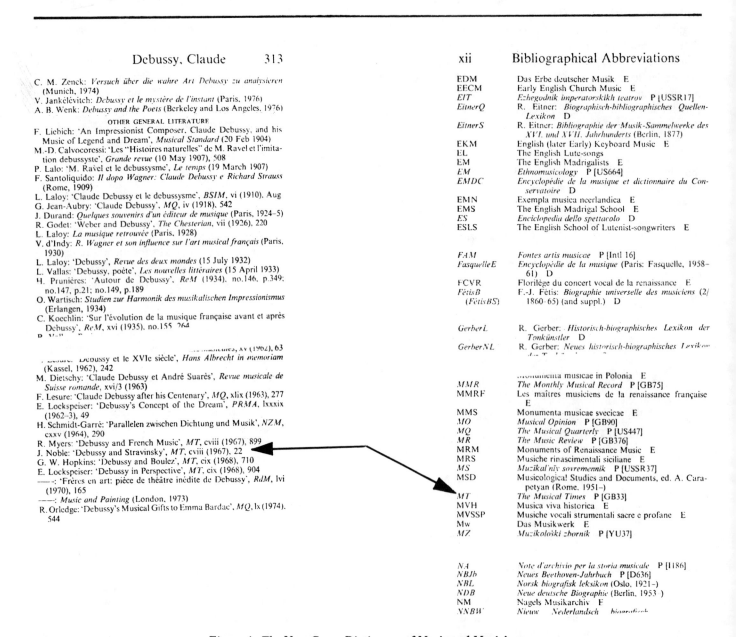

**Figure 4. The New Grove Dictionary of Music and Musicians.**

whether to look for more information about Debussy and Stravinsky, with the hope that you will uncover a properly refined topic, or perhaps to seek out another aspect of the life and works of the French composer. You are inclined to choose the former course of action but would like to have some further confirmation that the connection between the two composers is substantial.

*Textbooks and Specialized Reference Works*

Do not overlook the possibility that a textbook may shed some light on the topic you are contemplating. For example, Donald Jay Grout, in *A History of Western Music*, 3d ed. (New York: W.W. Norton, 1980), includes Stravinsky in a list of composers "who at one time or another came under his [Debussy's] influence" (p. 677). In *Exploring Twentieth-Century Music* (New York: Holt, Rinehart, and Winston, 1968), Otto Deri puts the case as follows (p. 165): "One can state without exaggeration that Debussy exerted the most important influence on a host of composers, including Stravinsky, Bartók, Berg, and even Webern and Boulez." And in Eric Salzman's *Twentieth-Century Music: An Introduction*, 2d ed. (Englewood Cliffs, NJ: Prentice-Hall, 1974), you read that "Stravinsky's first important works were written under the influence of his teacher, Rimsky-Korsakov, tempered by a little Debussy and a decidedly original and volatile imagination" (p. 28).

Dictionaries and encyclopedias of a specialized nature may also lend assistance. For example, the signed article (by Paul Jacobs) on Debussy in the *Dictionary of Contemporary Music*, edited by John Vinton (New York: E.P. Dutton, 1974), contains further information (pp. 177–179) about the influence factor; this strengthens your resolve to continue the present line of inquiry.

**Your Best Reference Resource?**

If you encounter any difficulties in locating materials in your library or in deciding which materials will meet your needs, do not hesitate to consult your reference librarian. Most large libraries will have one or more librarians with special subject training to help guide you through the bibliographical labyrinth of reference resources and to offer advice about search strategy. Libraries are complex institutions, and principles of using a library with efficiency are not necessarily self-evident. It usually takes a while to get over the feeling that you are *supposed* to learn everything about using a library through observation and deduction. You should not feel that you are somehow deficient if you ask for reference assistance. Your reference librarian — possibly your best reference resource — is there to help.

**Summary**

1. If you have the opportunity, choose a topic that you know something about already, one that interests you.
2. Do some reading in a standard dictionary or encyclopedia in order to find out more about the topic; locate discussions which summarize the material with which you are dealing.
3. Measure the breadth of the topic; begin to narrow it down if necessary.
4. Ask questions and see if they provide any useful leads.
5. Consult textbooks and specialized reference works to help determine if you are going in the right direction.
6. Do not fail to acquaint yourself with the services of your reference librarian.

"Choose a subject, ye who
write, suited to your
strength."
– Horace (from *Ars Poetica*).

## An Evolutionary Process

Choosing a suitable topic for a term paper is not necessarily — not usually, even — a matter of sudden inspiration. It is, rather, an evolutionary process which begins with a somewhat general subject area and leads step-by-step to a specific topic, one which is consonant with your own interests and background. Consider the case of Beethoven: "The main theme of the first movement in the Seventh Symphony is found only after six pages of untiring efforts. Six pages of trying, rejecting, testing."[1]

With the aid of selected reference tools, your topic has thus far been narrowed to "Aspects of Debussy and Stravinsky." In bringing Stravinsky into the picture, your intent is not to combine the life and works of both composers, of course, but to explore their relationship, their mutual influences (if they exist), and possibly even their opinions of each other.

## Measuring the Depth of Your Topic

At some point early in the topic refinement stage, it is beneficial to apply a set of criteria to measure the depth of your topic. (You will recall that criteria to measure the breadth of your topic were discussed in Chapter 1.) These criteria should help to determine whether or not your topic is "tailor-made" for you:

1. Language(s) of source materials.
2. Special skills (besides language skills) or knowledge outside the discipline of music.
3. Advanced analytical techniques.
4. Notation and performance practice.

Some amplification of these four points is in order:
1. Foreign language skills remain essential for much musical research of an historical nature, even though English sources for many topics are plentiful and authoritative. As time passes, more and more translations of foreign language materials, particularly in the area of theoretical treatises, are likely to be available. But at present, in order to do a thorough job of research on any given topic, it is not unlikely that you will have to deal with some foreign language materials. For example, for composers of international stature such as Debussy and Stravinsky, you will find major sources in French, German, and Italian.

Do not despair, though, if your foreign language background is not strong. Many of the roman alphabet foreign works in your library do not require great fluency in the language in order to make use of the information given. It may even be possible to glean some essentials if you read a closely related language. For example, if you read Italian, you may be able to make use of the Spanish *Diccionario de la música Labor*, edited by Joaquín Pena and Higinio Anglés (Barcelona: Labor, 1954; 2 vols.), or, if you have a knowledge of German, the Dutch *Encyclopedie van de muziek*, edited by L.M.G. Arntzenius and others (Amsterdam: Elsevier, 1956–57; 2 vols.) may yield some facts.

2. Certain subject areas within the sphere of music require special non-musical skills or knowledge as a prerequisite for research. The acoustics of musical instruments, for example, is practically in the domain of physics and mathematics, and acoustical research materials abound with advanced mathematical formulae. Music therapy as a discipline places considerable emphasis on aspects of psychology and physiology. And for certain projects in music education, particularly those dealing with the evaluation of tests or questionnaires, a knowledge of elementary statistics may be necessary.

3. The analysis of many twentieth-century compositions requires a thorough grounding in serial or other complex compositional techniques. A perusal of some of the remarkably erudite articles in the journal *Perspectives of New Music* (Princeton, NJ: Princeton University Press, 1962– ) will confirm this fact. Early music, too, requires special analytical techniques, as the *Journal of the American Musicological Society* (Richmond, VA: American Musicological Society, 1948– ) frequently shows.

4. The notation of music before 1600, generally speaking, and that employed by some composers of the present day, both require special study. For the early period, consult Willi Apel, *The Notation of Polyphonic Music, 900-1600*, 5th ed. (Cambridge, MA: Medieval Academy of America, 1961); and for today's music, Erhard Karkoschka, *Notation in New Music: A Critical Guide to Interpretation and Realisation* (New York: Praeger, 1972), is a good text. Perfor-

---

[1]Frederick Dorian, in *The Beethoven Companion*, ed. by Thomas K. Sherman and Louis Biancolli (Garden City, NY: Doubleday, 1972), p. 494.

mance practice, that is, the study of early performance techniques and the authentic performance of early music on original instruments or faithful reproductions, requires special attention to historical treatises, details concerning the notation of early manuscripts and prints, and the construction and tuning of early instruments. Robert Donington, author of *The Interpretation of Early Music*, new version (New York: St. Martin's, 1974), is a prominent authority on this subject.

If you have trouble with foreign language materials, your reference librarian or professor may be able to help you over the roughest spots. At least, be persistent; you may find that your difficulties are not so formidable as you thought at first glance.

### The First Foreign Language Hurdles

At present, German is the foreign language most frequently needed for musical research. For materials in German, a handy dictionary of musical terminology is *Langenscheidts Fachwörterbuch: Musik*, by Horst Leuchtmann and Philippine Schick (Berlin: Langenscheidt, 1964); both English-German and German-English equivalents are listed.

One of the most comprehensive and scholarly music encyclopedias now available is *Die Musik in Geschichte und Gegenwart*, edited by Friedrich Blume (Kassel: Bärenreiter-Verlag, 1949– ). Fourteen volumes covering the alphabet from A–Z, plus the two supplementary volumes (1973, 1979) listing corrections and additions, have appeared thus far; an index has been announced by the publisher. *MGG*, as it is often called, is lavishly illustrated and contains articles by well-known scholars from around the world. To cite *MGG* in your term paper is to cite a work of acknowledged excellence.

There are several important aspects of *MGG* that you should keep in mind. First of all, the basic set of fourteen volumes was published serially over a span of two decades. The information in the later volumes, therefore, is considerably more up-to-date than that in the earlier ones. For example, the article on Debussy is found in volume three, published in 1954; in contrast, the article on Stravinsky, in volume twelve, was not published until 1965. (It should be noted that *The New Grove* is different in this respect: its twenty volumes were published simultaneously.) At the beginning of every volume, you will find a list of *Abkürzungen* (abbreviations), which is practically indispensable for deciphering the heavily abbreviated text. (See FIGURE 5.) The text is set in densely packed double columns; it may be helpful to have a magnifying glass handy!

Debussy is covered in slightly more than fourteen and one-half columns (vol. 3, cols. 62–77) — not an especially long article for a major composer in *MGG*. As in the case of other articles of similar scope on a single composer, there is a biographical section followed by a classified list of works, after which is found a discussion of the works and a partially annotated bibliography.

This bibliography — one of the most extensive thus far encountered — cites books, parts of books (a noteworthy feature, not found in many bibliographies of this kind), periodical articles, doctoral dissertations, and publications of correspondence. Unhappily, on the subject of Debussy and Stravinsky, nothing of great consequence is evident. But, a biography of Debussy by W. Danckert, pointed out in FIGURE 5, is reported to have an exceptionally complete bibliography; this fact should be recorded for future reference.

Scouring a bibliography such as the one in the *MGG* article may seem like a trial. If you are not used to this kind of work, you may want to fling up your hands in desperation: after all the searching, you still have not found a citation that is precisely what you want. The old-fashioned quality of perseverance must be brought to bear here. According to André Gide, the French writer, "To win one's joy through struggle is better than to yield to melancholy."[2]

### Another Success

Another first-rate German reference work is the *Riemann Musik Lexikon*, 12th ed., edited by Wilibald Gurlitt (Mainz: B. Schott's Söhne, 1959–1975; 5 vols.). Like *Baker's* and *The New Grove*, this publication still bears the name of its first editor, who in this case was Hugo Riemann (1849–1919), a prolific and influential scholar. The three basic volumes — two of biography, one of terminology and topics — have been supplemented by two further volumes of biography. The bibliographical references are very numerous and up-to-date.

The article on Debussy in volume one (pp. 376–377) has only about thirty-four references, but the comparable article in the first supplementary volume (pp. 264–265) has about four times that many. In the latter, the book *Avec Stravinsky* (*With Stravinsky*; Monaco, 1958) is cited; according to the annotation, it contains some hitherto unpublished letters by Debussy. This is a promising reference, of course, but an even more promising one, as you can see in FIGURE 6, is found in the article on Stravinsky in the second supplementary volume (pp. 745–749): A. Souris, "Debussy et Stravinsky," *Revue Belge de Musicologie*, volume 16 (1962).

"Debussy and Stravinsky!" Now is the time for celebration. The Souris article is yet another piece of writing directly linking the two composers that you have come upon, and it is possible that it may give you some ideas about further refinement of your topic. Here again, even if you do not read French, you may find some useful bibliographical references lurking about.

---

[2]André Gide, *Journals*, May 12, 1927, tr. Justin O'Brien (New York: Vintage Books, 1956), vol. 2, p. 21.

# A B K Ü R Z U N G E N

Die Abkürzungen gelten im allgemeinen auch für die Mehrzahl der betreffenden Wörter

| | | | |
|---|---|---|---|
| A. | = Alt, Alto | Ebg. | = Eulenburg, Leipzig |
| Abb. | = Abbildung | ed., edd. | = edidit, ediderunt |
| Abdr., Abschr. | = Abdruck, Abschrift | EdM | = das Erbe deutsch. Musik 1935 f. |
| Abt. | = Abteilung | einger. | = eingerichtet |
| AfMf | = Archiv für Musikforschung | Einl. | = Einleitung |
| AfMw | = Archiv für Musikwissenschaft | EitnerBg | = Eitner, Bibliographie der |
| ahd. | = althochdeutsch | | Musiksammelwerke |
| Ak., ak. | = Akustik, akustisch | EitnerQ | = Eitner, Biographisch-Biblio- |
| Akad., akad. | = Akademie, akademisch | | graphisches Quellenlexikon |
| AMl | = Acta Musicologica | engl. | = englisch |
| AmZ | = Allgemeine musikal. Zeitung | erl., ersch., erw. | = erläutert, erschienen, erweitert |
| AMz | = Allgemeine Musikzeitung | ev. | = evangelisch |
| Anh. | = Anhang | | |
| Anm. | = Anmerkung | Facs. | = Facsimile, Faksimile |
| anon. | = anonym | FétisB | = Fétis Biographie universelle |
| AR | = Antiphonale Romanum | Fg. | = Fagott |
| Ästh., ästh. | = Ästhetik, ästhetisch | Fischb. | = Fischbacher, Paris |
| Aufl., Ausg., Ausw. | = Auflage, Ausgabe, Auswahl | Fl. | = Flöte |
| AW | = Ausgewählte Werke | fortgef., fortges. | = fortgeführt, fortgesetzt |
| | | Forts. | = Fortsetzer, Fortsetzung |
| B., Bar., Bc. | = Baß, Bariton, Basso continuo | frz. | = französisch |
| B. & H. | = Breitkopf & Härtel, Wiesba- | Fs. | = Festschrift |
| | den und Leipzig | | |
| Bd., Bde. | = Band, Bände | GA | = Gesamtausgabe |
| Bearb., bearb. | = Bearbeiter, -ung, bearbeitet | Gb. | = Generalbaß |
| Begl. | = Begleitung | gemCh. | = gemischter Chor |
| Beih. IMG | = Beihefte d. Internat. Musikges. | Gerber ATL | = Gerber, Hist ... |
| Beil. | = Beilage | | |
| Beitr. | = Beitrag, Beiträge | Gerber NTL | |
| Bibl. | = Bibliothek | | |
| Bl. | = Blatt, Blätter | | |
| Bln. | = Berlin | | |
| Br. | = Bratsche | | |
| bulg. | = bulg... | | |
| Bull. | | | |

**Figure 5. Die Musik in Geschichte und Gegenwart.**

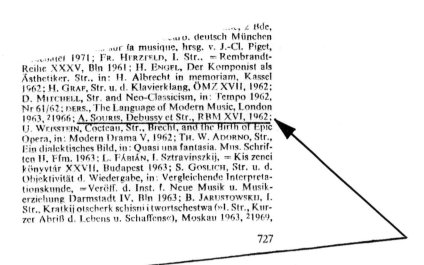

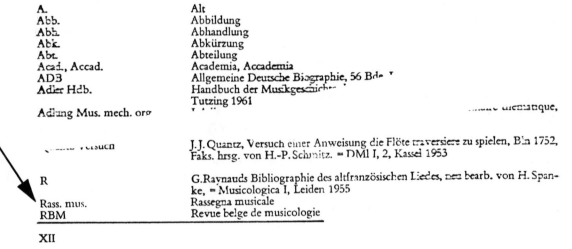

..., 2 Bde,
..., u. deutsch München
... aur la musique, hrsg. v. J.-Cl. Piget,
...châtel 1971; FR. HERZFELD, I. Str., = Rembrandt-
Reihe XXXV, Bln 1961; H. ENGEL, Der Komponist als
Ästhetiker. Str., in: H. Albrecht in memoriam, Kassel
1962; H. GRAF, Str. u. d. Klavierklang, ÖMZ XVII, 1962;
D. MITCHELL, Str. and Neo-Classicism, in: Tempo 1962,
Nr 61/62; DERS., The Language of Modern Music, London
1963, ²1966; A. SOURIS, Debussy et Str., RBM XVI, 1962;
U. WEISSTEIN, Cocteau, Str., Brecht, and the Birth of Epic
Opera, in: Modern Drama V, 1962; TH. W. ADORNO, Str.,
Ein dialektisches Bild, in: Quasi una fantasia. Mus. Schrif-
ten II. Ffm. 1963; L. FÁBIÁN, I. Sztravinszkij, = Kis zenei
könyvtár XXVII, Budapest 1963; S. GOSLICH, Str. u. d.
Objektivität d. Wiedergabe, in: Vergleichende Interpreta-
tionskunde, = Veröff. d. Inst. f. Neue Musik u. Musik-
erziehung Darmstadt IV, Bln 1963; B. JARUSTOWSKIJ, I.
Str., Kratkij otscherk schisni i twortschestwa (»I. Str., Kur-
zer Abriß d. Lebens u. Schaffens«), Moskau 1963, ²1969,

727

## Abkürzungen und Siglen

*Die Abkürzungen gelten jeweils für sämtliche Flexionsformen sowie fremdsprachliche Formen des betreffenden Wortes*

| | |
|---|---|
| A. | Alt |
| Abb. | Abbildung |
| Abh. | Abhandlung |
| Abk. | Abkürzung |
| Abt. | Abteilung |
| Acad., Accad. | Academia, Accademia |
| ADB | Allgemeine Deutsche Biographie, 56 Bde |
| Adler Hdb. | Handbuch der Musikgeschich... |
| | Tutzing 1961 |
| Adlung Mus. mech. org | ... thématique, |
| ... Versuch | J. J. Quantz, Versuch einer Anweisung die Flöte traversiere zu spielen, Bln 1752, Faks. hrsg. von H.-P. Schmitz. = DMI I, 2, Kassel 1953 |
| R | G. Raynauds Bibliographie des altfranzösischen Liedes, neu bearb. von H. Spanke, = Musicologica I, Leiden 1955 |
| Rass. mus. | Rassegna musicale |
| RBM | Revue belge de musicologie |

XII

Figure 6. Riemann Musik Lexikon.

## The Home Country

In order to round out your survey of foreign language encyclopedias and dictionaries of music, you should consult at least one French publication, since Debussy was French, of course, and Stravinsky, as well, was closely associated with French music. One occasionally finds that the best surveys of a composer's life and works emanate from that composer's native or adopted country. (Stravinsky lived in France from 1920 until 1939.)

A French publication strong in twentieth-century music is the *Encyclopédie de la musique*, published under the direction of François Michel in collaboration with François Lesure and Vladimir Féderov (Paris: Fasquelle, 1958–61; 3 vols.); it is sometimes called "Fasquelle," after the publisher. The well-illustrated article on Debussy (vol. 1, pp. 629--641) contains a reference to an essay by A. Schaeffner, "Debussy et ses rapports avec la musique russe" ("Debussy and His Connection with Russian Music"), in *Musique russe* (vol. 1, 1953), pointed out in FIGURE 7.

## Is Your Topic Established?

In Chapter 1, you learned about dealing with a topic which is too broad, one which involves too many sources

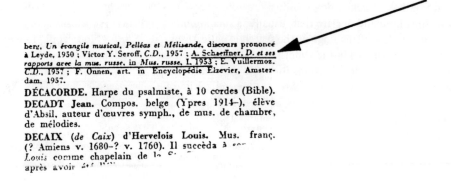

berg, Un évangile musical, Pelléas et Mélisande, discours prononcé
à Leyde, 1950 ; Victor Y. Seroff, C.D., 1957 ; A. Schaeffner, D. et ses
rapports avec la mus. russe, in Mus. russe, I, 1953 ; E. Vuillermoz,
C.D., 1957 ; F. Onnen, art. in Encyclopédie Elzevier, Amsterdam, 1957.

**DÉCACORDE.** Harpe du psalmiste, à 10 cordes (Bible).

**DECADT Jean.** Compos. belge (Ypres 1914–), élève
d'Absil, auteur d'œuvres symph., de mus. de chambre,
de mélodies.

**DECAIX** (de Caix) **d'Hervelois Louis.** Mus. franç.
(? Amiens v. 1680–? v. 1760). Il succéda à son
Louis comme chapelain de la c.
après avoir été m...

Figure 7.  Encyclopédie de la musique.  Paris:  Fasquelle, 1958--61.

---

to be considered for a term paper. Now, conversely, you must consider whether in fact you are going to have enough material to build upon. You certainly do not want to spend too much time on a topic that turns out to be "impoverished."

If you feel you have not negotiated the foreign language hurdles that have been presented in connection with the present topic, you may be in need of some bibliographical first aid. With such aid, you should expect complete recovery and even increased capability of continuing the search.

### Bibliographical First Aid

This kind of first aid is administered through the use of one or more special bibliographies. Consult your reference librarian in order to determine if there are any closely related to the topic you are considering. Later on, in Chapter 5, bibliographies and how to locate them will be discussed more thoroughly.

Luckily, there are two extensive bibliographies which fill the present need: (1) Claude Abravanel, *Claude Debussy: A Bibliography* (Detroit: Information Coordinators, 1974); and (2) Carroll D. Wade, "A Selected Bibliography of Igor Stravinsky," in *Stravinsky: A New Appraisal of His Work*, edited by Paul Henry Lang (New York: W.W. Norton, 1963, pp. 97–109). In the first, under the heading "Literature on the Relations of Debussy: Musicians," there are seven articles which link the names of the two composers, and two of these are in English, as you can see in FIGURE 8. The second bibliography lists one relevant article, in German, which is also cited in Abravanel.

---

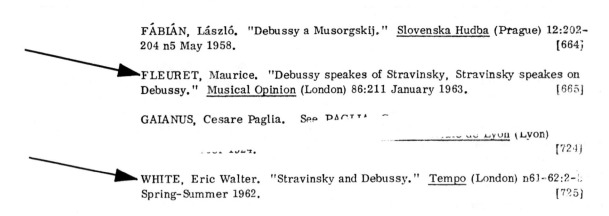

FÁBIÁN, László.  "Debussy a Musorgskij."  Slovenska Hudba (Prague) 12:202-204 n5 May 1958.                                                                                   [664]

FLEURET, Maurice.  "Debussy speakes of Stravinsky, Stravinsky speakes on Debussy."  Musical Opinion (London) 86:211 January 1963.                        [665]

GAIANUS, Cesare Paglia.  See PAGLIA ...

                                                    ... de Lyon (Lyon)
                                                                                                            [724]

WHITE, Eric Walter.  "Stravinsky and Debussy."  Tempo (London) n61-62:2-5 Spring-Summer 1962.                                                                                      [725]

Figure 8.  Abravanel, Claude.  Claude Debussy:  A Bibliography.

Does it require a "leap of faith" to continue with a topic on which you have tracked down only a few references? Let us go out on a limb and declare that, usually, a small number of pertinent articles at this stage of the search is indicative of sufficient source material in the wider sphere of literature for a term paper. The book literature, for example, remains to be searched via the card catalog. And the periodical literature, as well, has not been thoroughly covered. Much remains to be done. But your topic is still sound, thanks to some bibliographical first aid.

### Engraved in Stone?

As you go further, do not hesitate to narrow your topic even more if necessary. At no point are you obliged to consider your topic engraved in stone. As it stands now, your topic is "Debussy and Stravinsky: Relationship and Influences." Practical circumstances, such as the availability (or non-availability) of sources, may require some changes. Allow your topic to evolve according to your own interests and abilities.

### Summary

1. Measure the depth of your topic to find out if you have the background to deal with it.
2. Important source materials in music are not infrequently in foreign languages.
3. If necessary, seek help in finding one or more special bibliographies on your topic or closely related to it.
4. Your topic can be further modified if conditions dictate.

## A Tool with Limitations

The card catalog is the most valuable key to your library's collections.[1] But because it must differentiate and classify all the materials represented within its drawers, it has attained a degree of complexity, especially in large libraries, that can be truly intimidating to those who do not have very much experience using it. To those who have uncovered some or most of its secrets — we suspect no one has uncovered *all* of them — it can be simply frustrating on occasion because of some of the things it does *not* do.

The card catalog does not provide an index to everything in the library. For example, it does not provide an index of periodical articles. You must go to periodical indexes to find classified listings of individual articles. Pamphlets and other ephemeral materials, as well as government documents, are seldom represented within its drawers. It does not evaluate materials. You must search for reviews in the periodical literature and other sources.

There is yet another frustration: the subject headings listed in the card catalog may, for the most part, be too broad for your purposes. (Even so, a sophisticated approach to subject headings, as we shall see later, can be a significant aid to research.)

Basically, one must not expect too much from the card catalog.

## The Personal Name Approach

Since your topic has been narrowed down to two individuals, Debussy and Stravinsky, you should have no difficulty in locating some pertinent references in the card catalog, because a book *by* or *about* either composer will be listed under the personal name. In a dictionary catalog (i.e., one in which all cards are filed in a continuous sequence, as are entries in a dictionary), books *about* a person are generally filed in a separate alphabetic sequence right after books *by* that person. In a divided catalog (i.e., one in which there are two or possibly more sequences according to type of entry),

---

[1]Unless, of course, your library has some other kind of index, such as a book catalog, microform catalog, or an online computer catalog.

books *about* a person will be filed in the subject segment of the catalog, while books *by* a person will be filed in another. Many divided catalogs have a separate sequence for subject entries and another for all other entries — author, title, etc. But whether you are using a dictionary or divided catalog, be assured that the personal name approach is a good one.

Separate chapters in books, as for example a single chapter on Stravinsky in a text on contemporary music, are not usually listed in the card catalog. Parts larger than a chapter, as in the case of the section devoted to Stravinsky in *Perspectives on Schoenberg and Stravinsky*, rev. ed., edited by Benjamin Boretz and Edward T. Cone (New York: W.W. Norton, 1972), are sometimes entered in the card catalog under the personal name subject heading (see FIGURE 9). However, parts of books written, edited, or illustrated by a person are often found as personal name added entries. This is true with regard to Debussy and some of his unedited letters (*"lettres inédites de Claude Debussy"*) published in *Avec Stravinsky*, as shown in FIGURE 9. (In library terminology, the names and subjects at the bottom of a catalog card are called tracings; those given arabic numerals are the subject headings and those with roman numerals, mostly titles, joint authors, and editors, are called added entries.)

Personal names are easily found in the card catalog, but what about subjects that are not personal names, such as, say, "Contemporary Music in France?" It is extremely unlikely that you will find a subject heading such as this in your card catalog. Instead, you may discover MUSIC — FRANCE — HISTORY AND CRITICISM (see FIGURE 9).

## An Important Guide to Subject Headings

You may be somewhat dismayed by having to use a subject heading that seems more cumbersome or less specific than the one you had in mind. If so, you should be aware that librarians hardly ever make up their own subject headings. Most of them accept the subject headings and regulations governing their use in *Library of Congress Subject Headings*, 9th ed. (Washington, DC: Library of Congress, 1980). This hefty two-volume compilation is continually being revised and updated by means of printed supplements. It is useful to the researcher and indispensable to the librarian.

Imagine what it would be like if there were no standards

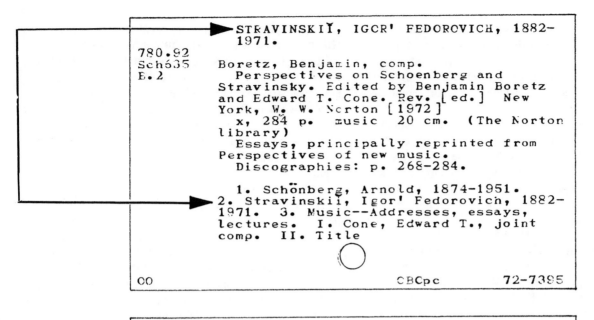

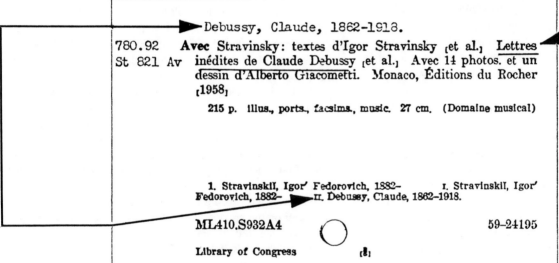

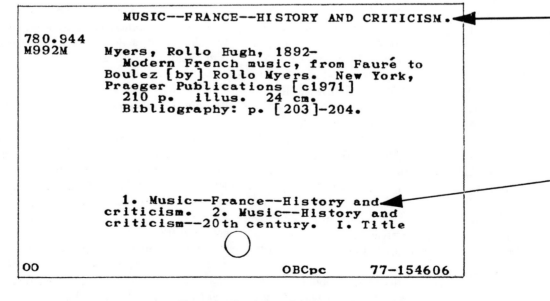

Figure 9. Catalog cards.

or controls! With librarians across the country inventing countless subject headings with varying degrees of interchangeability, one would have to learn a different set of guidelines for subject headings in every library visited. Most would agree that this uncontrolled state of affairs would be extraordinarily impractical.

Fortunately, the Library of Congress guide to subject headings can be made available to you, and by becoming somewhat familiar with it, you will be able to make your search more efficient. But, like the card catalog, it is not without complexities, and you may want to enlist the aid of your reference librarian if you have not used this tool before. In the Library of Congress guide you will find, for example, that even though FRENCH LITERATURE is there in boldfaced type — an indication that it is a valid subject heading — no comparable heading for "French music" exists. The correct form for the latter subject is MUSIC, FRENCH. Alas, you will not find MUSIC, FRENCH in the guide either, but its validity can be deduced from the existence of the following heading: "Music, African [Brazilian, German, etc.]," shown in FIGURE 10. The point is this: while certain generalizations can be made, others cannot. Close observation of representative headings, such as the one just mentioned, will help you to determine what headings are likely to be found in your library's catalog.

What about Debussy and Stravinsky? What subjects other than personal names would be applicable in this case? We can consider the chronological side of the question first of all and begin looking for subjects related to the contemporary period. In scanning the broad subject heading MUSIC and its subdivisions, shown in part in FIGURE 10, we come to MUSIC — HISTORY AND CRITICISM — 20TH CENTURY, which, although fairly broad, should prove useful. Directly underneath is an "sa" ("see also") reference to IMPRESSIONISM (MUSIC), another valid heading which might yield some pertinent citations in the card catalog. The latter is to be distinguished from "Modern music," shown a little further down, which is preceded by an "x" ("see from"). The "x" indicates that this is *not* a valid heading, but one from which a "see" reference in the card catalog is made. In other words, you will *not* find books listed under "Modern music," but rather a cross reference which tells you to look under MUSIC — HISTORY AND CRITICISM — 20TH CENTURY (see FIGURE 11).

There is another type of cross reference, indicated by "xx" ("see also from"). For example, under MUSIC — HISTORY AND CRITICISM — MEDIEVAL, 400–1500 is a heading CHURCH MUSIC — HISTORY AND CRITICISM (see FIGURE 10). The "xx" before the latter heading indicates that it *is* used, and that it is one from which a "see also" cross reference in the catalog can be made (see FIGURE 11). By looking up the related "xx" headings in the card catalog, you increase your chances of finding pertinent materials.

You should also check on the library's holdings under MUSIC with various geographical subdivisions plus the fur-

ther subdivision — HISTORY AND CRITICISM, such as MUSIC — FRANCE — HISTORY AND CRITICISM. The heading MUSIC — RUSSIA — HISTORY AND CRITICISM would be appropriate for material concerning the early period of Stravinsky and perhaps for Debussy in connection with his visits to Russia in the entourage of Mme. von Meck. However, since these subject headings are very broad, you must not expect that every book (or even most books) listed under them will contain information related to your present topic.

After considering the chronological and geographical aspects of your topic, you might approach it through headings covering some of the major kinds of compositions by Debussy and Stravinsky. For example, you might decide to look up DANCE MUSIC — HISTORY AND CRITICISM or perhaps OPERA — HISTORY AND CRITICISM (both shown without the subdivision as "see also" references under MUSIC in FIGURE 10). Under these headings, you are likely to find surveys of music literature.

Finally, be on the look-out for the subdivision — BIBLIOGRAPHY, which is valid in connection with most subject headings, whether they are personal names or not. At this stage of your search, a ready-made bibliography on some aspect of your topic can save you much time and effort, especially if it is comprehensive and up-to-date. Two important bibliographies closely related to the present topic were mentioned in the "bibliographical first aid" section of Chapter 2: Abravanel on Debussy and Wade on Stravinsky. FIGURE 12 shows a subject-heading entry for the first of these. If you do not find a heading with the subdivision — BIBLIOGRAPHY, check carefully in the card catalog under the subjects you are concerned with to see if a bibliography is indicated in a note on any of the catalog cards. We find such a note on an entry for the Danckert biography of Debussy, mentioned in Chapter 2 (see FIGURES 5 and 13).

The *Library of Congress Subject Headings* has many complexities; they have not all been covered here. In the course of writing your term paper, you will not of course be expected to become absolutely proficient in the use of this tool, but some familiarity with it will help you to use the card catalog more effectively.

## Preliminary Evaluation

After having succeeded in finding some appropriate subject headings, and having located a number of references to books, you are now about to leave the card catalog and set out for the stacks. You have noted on your growing collection of file cards the call numbers of the books you want to consult and other significant information gleaned from catalog entries.

If your library has an extensive music collection, the card catalog may cite a larger number of seemingly germane titles than you will be able to use for your term paper. (If you had chosen a topic on Wagner or Beethoven, you would

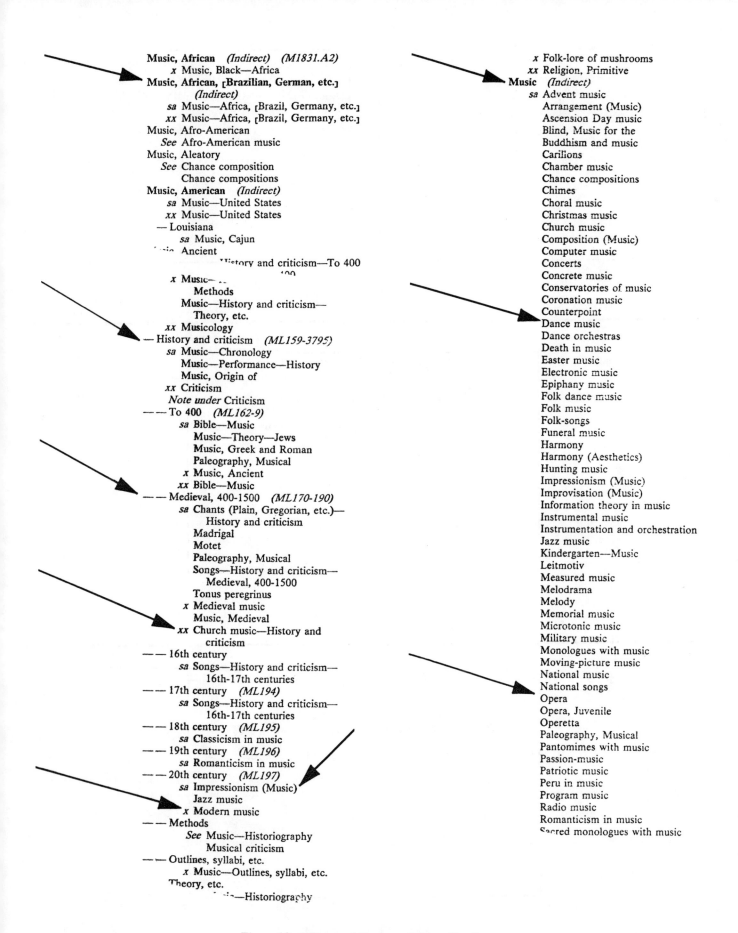

**Music, African** *(Indirect)* *(M1831.A2)*
    *x* Music, Black—Africa
**Music, African, ₁Brazilian, German, etc.₁**
    *(Indirect)*
    *sa* Music—Africa, ₁Brazil, Germany, etc.₁
    *xx* Music—Africa, ₁Brazil, Germany, etc.₁
Music, Afro-American
    *See* Afro-American music
Music, Aleatory
    *See* Chance composition
    Chance compositions
**Music, American** *(Indirect)*
    *sa* Music—United States
    *xx* Music—United States
 — Louisiana
    *sa* Music, Cajun
 — Ancient
    History and criticism—To 400
        400
   *x* Music—..
    Methods
    Music—History and criticism—
      Theory, etc.
  *xx* Musicology
— History and criticism *(ML159-3795)*
    *sa* Music—Chronology
    Music—Performance—History
    Music, Origin of
  *xx* Criticism
  *Note under* Criticism
——— To 400 *(ML162-9)*
    *sa* Bible—Music
    Music—Theory—Jews
    Music, Greek and Roman
    Paleography, Musical
   *x* Music, Ancient
  *xx* Bible—Music
——— Medieval, 400-1500 *(ML170-190)*
    *sa* Chants (Plain, Gregorian, etc.)—
      History and criticism
    Madrigal
    Motet
    Paleography, Musical
    Songs—History and criticism—
      Medieval, 400-1500
    Tonus peregrinus
   *x* Medieval music
    Music, Medieval
  *xx* Church music—History and
      criticism
——— 16th century
    *sa* Songs—History and criticism—
      16th-17th centuries
——— 17th century *(ML194)*
    *sa* Songs—History and criticism—
      16th-17th centuries
——— 18th century *(ML195)*
    *sa* Classicism in music
——— 19th century *(ML196)*
    *sa* Romanticism in music
——— 20th century *(ML197)*
    *sa* Impressionism (Music)
    Jazz music
   *x* Modern music
——— Methods
    *See* Music—Historiography
    Musical criticism
——— Outlines, syllabi, etc.
   *x* Music—Outlines, syllabi, etc.
  Theory, etc.
    ——Historiography

   *x* Folk-lore of mushrooms
  *xx* Religion, Primitive
**Music** *(Indirect)*
    *sa* Advent music
    Arrangement (Music)
    Ascension Day music
    Blind, Music for the
    Buddhism and music
    Carillons
    Chamber music
    Chance compositions
    Chimes
    Choral music
    Christmas music
    Church music
    Composition (Music)
    Computer music
    Concerts
    Concrete music
    Conservatories of music
    Coronation music
    Counterpoint
    Dance music
    Dance orchestras
    Death in music
    Easter music
    Electronic music
    Epiphany music
    Folk dance music
    Folk music
    Folk-songs
    Funeral music
    Harmony
    Harmony (Aesthetics)
    Hunting music
    Impressionism (Music)
    Improvisation (Music)
    Information theory in music
    Instrumental music
    Instrumentation and orchestration
    Jazz music
    Kindergarten—Music
    Leitmotiv
    Measured music
    Melodrama
    Melody
    Memorial music
    Microtonic music
    Military music
    Monologues with music
    Moving-picture music
    National music
    National songs
    Opera
    Opera, Juvenile
    Operetta
    Paleography, Musical
    Pantomimes with music
    Passion-music
    Patriotic music
    Peru in music
    Program music
    Radio music
    Romanticism in music
    Sacred monologues with music

Figure 10. Library of Congress Subject Headings.

CHURCH MUSIC--HISTORY AND CRITICISM

see also

MUSIC--HISTORY AND CRITICISM--MEDIEVAL, 400-1500

MODERN MUSIC

see

MUSIC--HISTORY AND CRITICISM--20TH CENTURY

Figure 11. Catalog cards.

Reference    DEBUSSY, CLAUDE, 1862-1918--
             BIBLIOGRAPHY
78 0.92
D354A    Abravanel, Claude
         Claude Debussy, a bibliography.
      Detroit, Information Coordinators,
      1974.
         214 p.  24cm.  (Detroit studies in
      music bibliography, 29)

         1. Debussy, Claude, 1862-1918--
      Bibliography  I. Series

OO                                    O BCpc

Figure 12. Catalog card.

          DEBUSSY, CLAUDE, 1862-1918.
780.92  Danckert, Werner, 1900-
D 354 Da    Claude Debussy.  Berlin, W. de Gruyter,
       1950.
          xvi, 248 p.  ports., facsim., music.  20ᵐ.

          Bibliography: p. 219-242.

Figure 13. Catalog card.

probably find the biographies and commentaries exceedingly numerous.) In such a case, it will be to your advantage to seek out the most authoritative and useful items at once. The card catalog can help, in a preliminary way. (There will be more on evaluation in a later chapter.)

First of all, consider the date of publication, which follows the place of publication and the publisher on the catalog card. A book published within the last five years — reprints excepted — is, obviously, more likely to contain the fruits of recent research than one published two or more decades ago. Even though the question of the date of publication is usually not as crucial in the humanities as in the natural sciences or social sciences, it is still worth considering.

The publisher should also be noted. As you use your library more and more, you will probably become familiar with a number of books which are frequently called for and held in high esteem. Among major publishers in the United States, W.W. Norton & Co. has undoubtedly contributed more of these titles than any other. Prentice-Hall has also published a significant number of important titles in music. With regard to reprints, Da Capo and Dover have consistently brought out editions of older books whose usefulness has remained largely undiminished. On the other side of the Atlantic, Bärenreiter-Verlag (Kassel, W. Germany) and Oxford University Press (London), among others, have produced some splendid works of music scholarship. In addition, a group of publishers which can generally be relied upon to issue works of laudable erudition are the university presses, such as Harvard, Yale, Indiana, and California. This list of important publishers of music literature is certainly not exhaustive, but it gives some indication of what to look for.

Another very important thing to weigh is the scholarly reputation of the author. Experience in the use of music libraries and music materials will teach you that certain authors' books, like those of certain publishers, are widely used and consistently appear in conspicuous places, such as the reserve shelf. Your professor will no doubt be able to advise you if you have any questions about a particular author.

## An Interpolation

Among those tools and resources that you will use in the course of preparing your paper, you may find that the card catalog presents the most problems. This index to the library's collections contains a multiplicity of subject headings and various other forms of entry whose purpose is not self-evident. There are also the complexities of the filing order — something barely touched upon in this guide.

In the not-too-distant future, the card catalog may be superseded by the computer, and all of us will have to learn a brand new set of guidelines for looking things up. But at present, in the vast majority of libraries, the catalog with its familiar 3 by 5 cards remains one of the most important tools for research. Again, if you have any difficulties in solving the mysteries of this or indeed any other reference tool, call upon your reference librarian for help; it is that person's responsibility to advise you in the interpretation of the library's resources.

## Browsing — A Scholarly Activity?

You will have an opportunity to test your preliminary evaluations of books made at the card catalog when you are browsing in the bookstacks. Although browsing may seem to be a casual and informal activity, it is actually a very significant part of your search. Occasionally, you may overlook an important book at the card catalog; conversely, some titles which look important from the catalog description will turn out to be less so. Browsing will turn up the tangible evidence for evaluation. In checking over the contents pages for pertinent chapter headings and in perusing appendices and bibliographies, you will be able to decide which books will be useful.

The shelves which contain concentrations of materials closely related to your topic should be inspected very carefully. With regard to biographical information, for example, you will want to check certain sections of the 780.92's in the Dewey classification or the ML 410's in the Library of Congress classification. If you have noted down the *entire call number* of the titles selected at the card catalog, then these sections will not be difficult to find. (Another advantage of having written down the entire call number is that you will have something to refer to if some of your selections are not in place on the shelves and have to be requested at the circulation desk.)

## Additional Background Reading

After locating what appear to be the major monographs or essays on your two composers, and before going on to examine the supplements to the card catalog described in the following chapters, you should probably do some additional background reading. From your examination of the card catalog and inspection of the shelves, you have identified the following as important sources: Edward Lockspeiser, *Debussy: His Life and Mind* (New York: Macmillan, 1962; 2 vols.), and Eric Walter White, *Stravinsky: The Composer and His Works,* 2d ed. (Berkeley: University of California Press, 1979). In Lockspeiser you find a whole chapter devoted to "Diaghilev and Stravinsky." (It was Sergei Diaghilev, director of the Russian ballet, who commissioned several of Stravinsky's most important early works, including *The Rite of Spring*.) FIGURE 14 shows Lockspeiser's contents page and a page from the index of volume 2. From White you learn that Stravinsky's veneration of Debussy was sufficient to prompt the dedication of Stravinsky's *Zvezdoliki*

# Contents

Figure 14.  Lockspeiser, Edward.  Debussy: His Life and Mind.  New York: Macmillan, 1962.

(alternately known as *Le Roi des étoiles*, or *The King of the Stars*) and his *Symphonies d'instruments à vent* (*Symphonies of Wind Instruments*) to the French master. The two composers, you also note, knew each other a comparatively short time, from 1910 — the year of the premiere performance of Stravinsky's *L'Oiseau de feu (The Fire-Bird)* — to the death of Debussy in 1918. Such information, indicative of the relationship of the two composers, should be entered, along with important quotations, in your personal card file.

## Summary

1. The card catalog is an important research tool, but it has limitations and complexities which may need to be explained by your reference librarian.

2. Personal names yield information rather easily in the card catalog.

3. Subject headings that are not personal names are more difficult to deal with than personal names but are quite useful. The *Library of Congress Subject Headings* should be consulted when you are making up your list of appropriate subject headings.

4. You can make a preliminary evaluation of materials cited in the card catalog by taking into consideration the author, publisher, and date of publication.

5. Browsing in the stacks may help you to locate materials overlooked at the card catalog or to assess more completely those titles which you have already identified.

6. Additional background in more important sources will prepare you for going on to tools which supplement the card catalog.

## Beyond the Card Catalog

You have learned from the preceding chapter that the card catalog, however imposing and complex, has some limitations. If you go to your writing directly from the card catalog without investigating some of its supplements, you will no doubt have neglected some important materials pertaining to your topic. It is therefore necessary to become acquainted with those reference resources which do some of the things the card catalog does *not* do — resources which analyze or index the contents of some books, which give you directions to evaluations or reviews of books, and which index the periodical literature.

## What Is a Periodical?

In library terminology, a "periodical" is a publication which is issued regularly (for example, weekly, monthly, quarterly, etc.). Also called journals (or, more popularly, "magazines"), periodicals fall within the general classification of serials, which are issued either regularly or irregularly in sequentially numbered parts. For example, *The Musical Quarterly* (New York: G. Schirmer, 1915– ) would normally be referred to as a periodical, whereas *The Music Forum* (New York: Columbia University Press, 1967– ), which began as an annual but which has appeared somewhat irregularly during the past few years, could be considered a serial.

## The Essential Index

The most valuable index to music periodicals, indeed one of the most useful reference tools you will have occasion to use, is *The Music Index* (Detroit: Information Coordinators, 1949– ). Like the *Readers' Guide*, it is a continuing publication. Over 300 periodicals, including most of the well-known scholarly music journals in English and those in the major European languages, are currently indexed in it. Also covered are doctoral dissertations in music listed in *Dissertation Abstracts International* (to be discussed in a later chapter) and musical articles in a small number of non-music periodicals, including *Saturday Review* and *Soviet Life*.

*The Music Index* appears in monthly issues with annual cumulations and employs a guide to subject headings (revised annually) somewhat similar to the *Library of Congress Subject Headings*, described in the last chapter. It lists reviews of books, performances, and recordings. You will find that the first of these will be especially important for evaluating source materials. (See the listing of a review in FIGURE 15.)

You can find citations under personal names, just as you did in the card catalog. In this case, a systematic method of proceeding would be to look up both Debussy and Stravinsky in *all* of the annual cumulations and those monthly supplements not yet cumulated. Some researchers prefer to work backwards chronologically in lengthy periodical indexes such as this one, in order to be able to deal with the most recent literature first.

As you get down to work on *The Music Index*, it will be obvious to you that the articles listed under each composer are quite plentiful. There are in fact far too many to deal with in the limited time available for the research on your paper. You will therefore have to be selective in your reading. The limitations brought to bear on your topic and the background reading you have done should act as a guide in the selection process. In this instance, you might want to look for articles which deal with one or more of the following subject areas:

1. The period 1910–1918, i.e., the early period of Stravinsky and the late period of Debussy.
2. Correspondence between the two composers or correspondence from one to a third party which mentions the other.
3. Published writings of either composer which mention the other.
4. The dedicated works:
   (a) *En blanc et noir* — Debussy to Stravinsky.
   (b) *Zvezdoliki (Le Roi des étoiles)* — Stravinsky to Debussy.
   (c) *Symphonies d'instruments à vent* — Stravinsky to Debussy.
5. Russian influence on Debussy; French influence on Stravinsky.

For the period 1949 through 1977, *The Music Index* lists at least five articles, including two in English, which mention both Debussy and Stravinsky in the title. The references in the annual cumulation for 1963 are especially notable. As FIGURE 15 shows, there is a separate key to

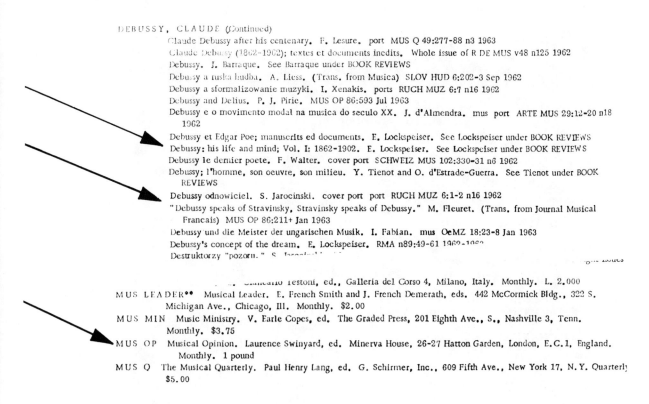

DEBUSSY, CLAUDE (Continued)

    Claude Debussy after his centenary. F. Lesure. port MUS Q 49:277-88 n3 1963
    Claude Debussy (1862-1962); textes et documents inedits. Whole issue of R DE MUS v48 n125 1962
    Debussy. J. Barraque. See Barraque under BOOK REVIEWS
    Debussy a ruska hudba. A. Liess. (Trans. from Musica) SLOV HUD 6:202-3 Sep 1962
    Debussy a sformalizowanie muzyki. I. Xenakis. ports RUCH MUZ 6:7 n16 1962
    Debussy and Delius. P. J. Pirie. MUS OP 86:593 Jul 1963
    Debussy e o movimento modal na musica do seculo XX. J. d'Almendra. mus port ARTE MUS 29:12-20 n18 1962
    Debussy et Edgar Poe; manuscrits ed documents. E. Lockspeiser. See Lockspeiser under BOOK REVIEWS
    Debussy: his life and mind; Vol. I: 1862-1902. E. Lockspeiser. See Lockspeiser under BOOK REVIEWS
    Debussy le dernier poete. F. Walter. cover port SCHWEIZ MUS 102:330-31 n6 1962
    Debussy; l'homme, son oeuvre, son milieu. Y. Tienot and O. d'Estrade-Guerra. See Tienot under BOOK REVIEWS
    Debussy odnowiciel. S. Jarocinski. cover port port RUCH MUZ 6:1-2 n16 1962
    "Debussy speaks of Stravinsky, Stravinsky speaks of Debussy." M. Fleuret. (Trans. from Journal Musical Francais) MUS OP 86:211+ Jan 1963
    Debussy und die Meister der ungarischen Musik. I. Fabian. mus OeMZ 18:23-8 Jan 1963
    Debussy's concept of the dream. E. Lockspeiser. RMA n89:49-61 1962-1963
    Destruktorzy "pozoru." S. Jarocinski.

                Giancarlo Testoni, ed., Galleria del Corso 4, Milano, Italy. Monthly. L. 2,000
MUS LEADER**   Musical Leader. E. French Smith and J. French Demerath, eds. 442 McCormick Bldg., 322 S. Michigan Ave., Chicago, Ill. Monthly. $2.00
MUS MIN   Music Ministry. V. Earle Copes, ed. The Graded Press, 201 Eighth Ave., S., Nashville 3, Tenn. Monthly. $3.75
MUS OP   Musical Opinion. Laurence Swinyard, ed. Minerva House, 26-27 Hatton Garden, London, E.C.1, England. Monthly. 1 pound
MUS Q   The Musical Quarterly. Paul Henry Lang, ed. G. Schirmer, Inc., 609 Fifth Ave., New York 17, N.Y. Quarterly $5.00

**Figure 15. The Music Index.**

---

abbreviations of the source titles. In *The Music Index*, as in many periodical indexes, this key is found at the beginning of each cumulated volume or separate issue.

### Prior to 1949

For the material from the period prior to 1949 — this date will soon become fixed in your mind as the starting point for *The Music Index* — it is sometimes helpful to search through one or more general indexes, for example, the *International Index* (New York: H.W. Wilson, 1907–65; predecessor of the *Social Sciences & Humanities Index*), or special indexes, such as the following: Eric Blom, *A General Index to Modern Musical Literature in the English Language* (London: J. Curwen & Sons, 1927), which covers the period 1915–26; *A Bibliography of Periodical Literature in Musicology* (Washington, DC: American Council of Learned Societies, 1940–43), a two-volume work which covers only 1938–40; and Ernest C. Krohn, *The History of Music: An Index to the Literature Available in a Selected Group of Musicological Publications* (St. Louis: Baton Music Co., 1958), which indexes 39 scholarly English and foreign language journals up to about 1951. An excerpt from the Krohn index, an especially useful work, is shown in FIGURE 16.

There are also indexes of long runs of single periodical titles, including these: Eric Blom and Jack A. Westrup, *Music and Letters: Index to Volumes I–XL* (1920–59) (London: Oxford University Press, 1962); Herbert K. Goodkind, *Cumulative Index to the Musical Quarterly, 1915–59* (New York: Goodkind Indexes, 1960) and its supplement for 1960–62 (New York: Goodkind Indexes, 1963). Finally, there are a small number of indexes which cover the articles of musical interest in a journal whose scope is broader than music alone. An example of this kind has been compiled by Arthur S. Wolff: *Speculum: An Index of Musically Related Articles and Book Reviews* (Ann Arbor, MI: Music Library Association, 1970). (Of course, this index would be of interest to you mainly if you were searching for medieval material; *Speculum* has the subtitle, *A Journal of Medieval Studies*.)

### The Latest News

Since *The Music Index* is about a year behind in its indexing at this point, for the most current periodical articles, you must rely on more general indexes, such as the *Readers' Guide* or the *Humanities Index* (New York: H.W. Wilson, 1974– ; an offshoot of the *Social Sciences & Humanities Index*), each of which indexes only a very small number of music periodicals. Somewhat stronger than these two in its coverage of music periodicals is the *British Humanities Index* (London: Library Association, 1963– ). Newspaper indexes,

SAMINSKY, Lazare
    Schönberg and Bartok, path-breakers.  MM 1:27-28.  F:1924.
    Bela Bartok and the graphic current in music.
    MQ 10:400-404.  1924.


                        Igor Stravinsky

ARMITAGE, Merle
    Igor Stravinsky.  MM 14:38.  1936.  BR: M. Bauer

BAUER, Marion
    Composite Stravinsky.  MM 14:38.  1936.

BLITZSTEIN, Marc
    The phenomenon of Stravinsky.  MQ 21:330-347.  1935.

BROWNE, Andrew J.
    Aspects of Stravinsky's work.  ML 11:360-366.  1930.

COEUROY, André
    Picasso and Stravinsky.  MM 5:3-8.  Ja:1928.

CHENNEVIERE, Rudhyar D.
    The two trends of modern music in Stravinsky's works.
    MQ 5:169-174.  1919.

COPLAND, Aaron
    From a composer's notebook:  Stravinsky.
    MM 6:15-19.  My:1929.

        ___, Frederick
                    ___ chronicles.  MM 13:51-53.  1935.
                        ___

Figure 16.  Krohn, Ernst C., comp.  The History of Music.  St. Louis:  Baton Music Co., 1958.

especially *The New York Times Index*, covering 1851 to date, (New York: New York Times, 1913– ), may also be useful for their citations of the most up-to-date material. FIGURE 17 traces information related to a recent Stravinsky festival in New York. Finally, you should be aware that some publishers of periodicals provide an index for each volume along with the last issue of that volume.

If you are interested in finding more tools of the kind mentioned in this section, a handy guide to consult is Joan M. Meggett, *Music Periodical Literature: An Annotated Bibliography of Indexes and Bibliographies* (Metuchen, NJ: Scarecrow, 1978).

## A Good Practice

It is a good practice to compile a rather complete list of *important* periodical articles in the early stages of your search, in fact, as soon as you have done enough background reading to get a good grasp of your topic. The reason is a practical one: your library may not have all the periodical articles you need; therefore, it may be necessary to request one or more articles through interlibrary loan, or you may have to make plans to visit another library.

## A Final Suggestion

Do not underestimate the importance of periodical indexes. The work of poring over volume after volume, of scanning hundreds of references, or of keeping in mind the chronological limitations of various tools may seem tedious, but it is absolutely essential. (At present, there is no single reference source or mechanism which controls or indexes the entire body of periodical literature concerning music. A great deal has already been accomplished through computer indexing, but no one seems to be predicting complete or comprehensive control in the near future.) If you become deeply enough involved with your topic, you may eventually regard these indexes as some of your stepping stones to success.

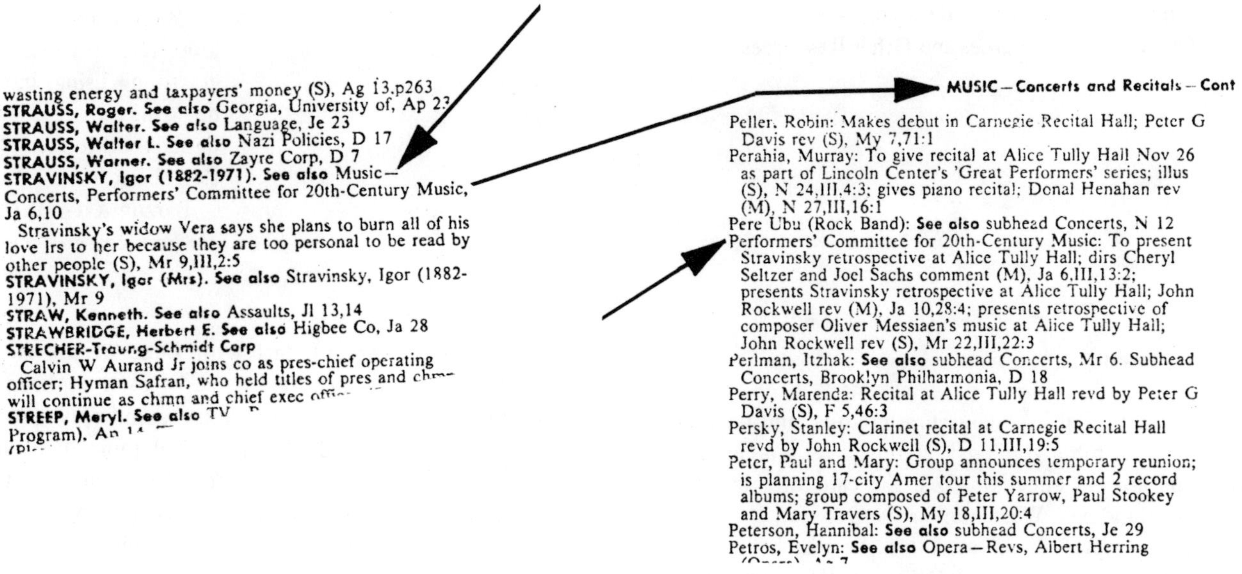

wasting energy and taxpayers' money (S), Ag 13.p263
**STRAUSS, Roger. See also** Georgia, University of, Ap 23
**STRAUSS, Walter. See also** Language, Je 23
**STRAUSS, Walter L. See also** Nazi Policies, D 17
**STRAUSS, Warner. See also** Zayre Corp, D 7
**STRAVINSKY, Igor (1882-1971). See also** Music—
Concerts, Performers' Committee for 20th-Century Music,
Ja 6,10
   Stravinsky's widow Vera says she plans to burn all of his
love lrs to her because they are too personal to be read by
other people (S), Mr 9,III,2:5
**STRAVINSKY, Igor (Mrs). See also** Stravinsky, Igor (1882-
1971), Mr 9
**STRAW, Kenneth. See also** Assaults, Jl 13,14
**STRAWBRIDGE, Herbert E. See also** Higbee Co, Ja 28
**STRECHER-Traung-Schmidt Corp**
   Calvin W Aurand Jr joins co as pres-chief operating
officer; Hyman Safran, who held titles of pres and chm
will continue as chmn and chief exec offi⌐
**STREEP, Meryl. See also** TV ⌐
Program). An ¹⁴
(⁻¹⌐

**MUSIC—Concerts and Recitals—Cont**

Peller, Robin: Makes debut in Carnegie Recital Hall; Peter G
   Davis rev (S), My 7,71:1
Perahia, Murray: To give recital at Alice Tully Hall Nov 26
   as part of Lincoln Center's 'Great Performers' series; illus
   (S), N 24,III,4:3; gives piano recital; Donal Henahan rev
   (M), N 27,III,16:1
Pere Ubu (Rock Band): **See also** subhead Concerts, N 12
Performers' Committee for 20th-Century Music: To present
   Stravinsky retrospective at Alice Tully Hall; dirs Cheryl
   Seltzer and Joel Sachs comment (M), Ja 6,III,13:2;
   presents Stravinsky retrospective at Alice Tully Hall; John
   Rockwell rev (M), Ja 10,28:4; presents retrospective of
   composer Oliver Messiaen's music at Alice Tully Hall;
   John Rockwell rev (S), Mr 22,III,22:3
Perlman, Itzhak: **See also** subhead Concerts, Mr 6. Subhead
   Concerts, Brooklyn Philharmonia, D 18
Perry, Marenda: Recital at Alice Tully Hall revd by Peter G
   Davis (S), F 5,46:3
Persky, Stanley: Clarinet recital at Carnegie Recital Hall
   revd by John Rockwell (S), D 11,III,19:5
Peter, Paul and Mary: Group announces temporary reunion;
   is planning 17-city Amer tour this summer and 2 record
   albums; group composed of Peter Yarrow, Paul Stookey
   and Mary Travers (S), My 18,III,20:4
Peterson, Hannibal: **See also** subhead Concerts, Je 29
Petros, Evelyn: **See also** Opera—Revs, Albert Herring
   ⌐⌐⌐⌐⌐⌐

Figure 17. The New York Times Index. (c) 1978 by The New York Times Company.
Reprinted by permission.

## Summary

1. For music, the most important periodical index is *The Music Index*, which began in 1949.
2. For citations from the period prior to 1949, it is necessary to consult a number of general and special indexes; the latest citations can be found in general indexes, including those of important newspapers.
3. If you find an overabundance of citations, your background reading should help you to determine which articles are most pertinent to your topic.
4. Compile a complete list of important periodical articles as soon as you have a good grasp of your topic.
5. Treat periodical indexes with respect (but not benign neglect). They can help you toward your goal.

" 'Bibliography is a rather loose term for research workers to be using, but there is no other that is as readily understood to mean 'information about books.' "
— Barzun & Graff (from *The Modern Researcher*)

## A Temptation

By now, you have chosen your topic and have gathered a number of bibliographical references by searching through dictionaries and encyclopedias, the card catalog, and major periodical indexes. What more is there to do?

The temptation to break off the search and enjoy the fruits already harvested may be great. If so, there is no harm in collecting your resources, making an assessment of their value, and perhaps drafting an outline. But be aware that there is more to the search stage — there are some important special bibliographies to consult. And as you make use of these bibliographies, it is helpful to distinguish among the following: (1) those pertaining to music literature, that is, writings on the subject of music, (2) those which list music scores only, and (3) those which list both music literature and music scores.

## The Bibliographical Overview

One of the most comprehensive guides to music bibliography and collateral resources is Vincent Duckles, *Music Reference and Research Materials: An Annotated Bibliography*, 3d ed. (New York: The Free Press, 1974). Over 1,900 items are cited and provided with descriptive annotations, some quite detailed. Reviews are listed for many of the more recent publications. The resources relating to your topic can easily be located through the subject index: Debussy is represented by an exposition catalog published by the Bibliothèque Nationale (see FIGURE 18) and Stravinsky by the Eric Walter White bio-bibliography, *Stravinsky: The Composer and His Works* (the second edition is mentioned in Chapter 3). Similar to Duckles is a series currently in progress: Guy A. Marco, *Information on Music: A Handbook of Reference Sources in European Languages* (Littleton, CO: Libraries Unlimited, 1975– ). See volume 1, *Basic and Universal Sources*, for its valuable suggestions concerning research methodology.

If you require help with general (i.e., non-musical) resources, such as general encyclopedias and bibliographies or guides to language and literature, you should look at Keith E. Mixter, *General Bibliography for Music Research*, 2d ed. (Detroit: Information Coordinators, 1975). Chapter X, "Indexes and Editions of Vocal Texts," might give you some

leads if you were to deal with some of the vocal works of Debussy and Stravinsky. It is good to keep in mind that general resources are quite commonly used in connection with research on a musical topic. Even if you do not actually incorporate material from such resources into your text, you may need them for clarifying or substantiating various points which deal peripherally or indirectly with music.

## Bibliographies of Music Literature

No harm can come from looking into that category of rarefied bibliographical materials called "bibliographies of bibliographies," or bibliographies which list only other bibliographies. Probably the best-known tool of this type is Theodore Besterman, *A World Bibliography of Bibliographies*, 4th ed. (Lausanne: Societas Bibliographica, 1965–66), published in five volumes. The music and drama section has been published separately as *Music and Drama; A Bibliography of Bibliographies* (Totowa, NJ: Rowman and Littlefield, 1971). Besterman cites a catalog of the works of Debussy as well as one of Stravinsky. The "classic" publication of this kind in the field of music is Marie Bobillier (Michel Brenet, pseudonym), "Bibliographie des bibliographies musicales," in *L'Année musicale*, vol. 3 (1913) pp. 1–152. Considering the date of this publication, it is somewhat remarkable that Debussy is included. As FIGURE 19 shows, he appears as the object of a bibliographical study in Octave Seré, *Musiciens français d'aujourd'hui (French Musicians of Today)* (Paris: Mercure de France, 1911). This publication is easily traced from the "see" reference ("voyez") under "Debussy." (Stravinsky is not included.)

In the realm of general bibliographies of music literature is *RILM Abstracts of Music Literature*, edited by Barry S. Brook (New York: International RILM Center, 1967– ). "RILM" (for *Répertoire internationale de littérature musicale*) is a comprehensive source for annotated citations of books and periodical articles from many countries. It appears quarterly — the fourth issue of each year is an index for that year — and is classified according to various broad headings, such as "historical musicology," "ethnomusicology," and "pedagogy," each of which is further subdivided. Computer technology has been applied to the system of indexing for

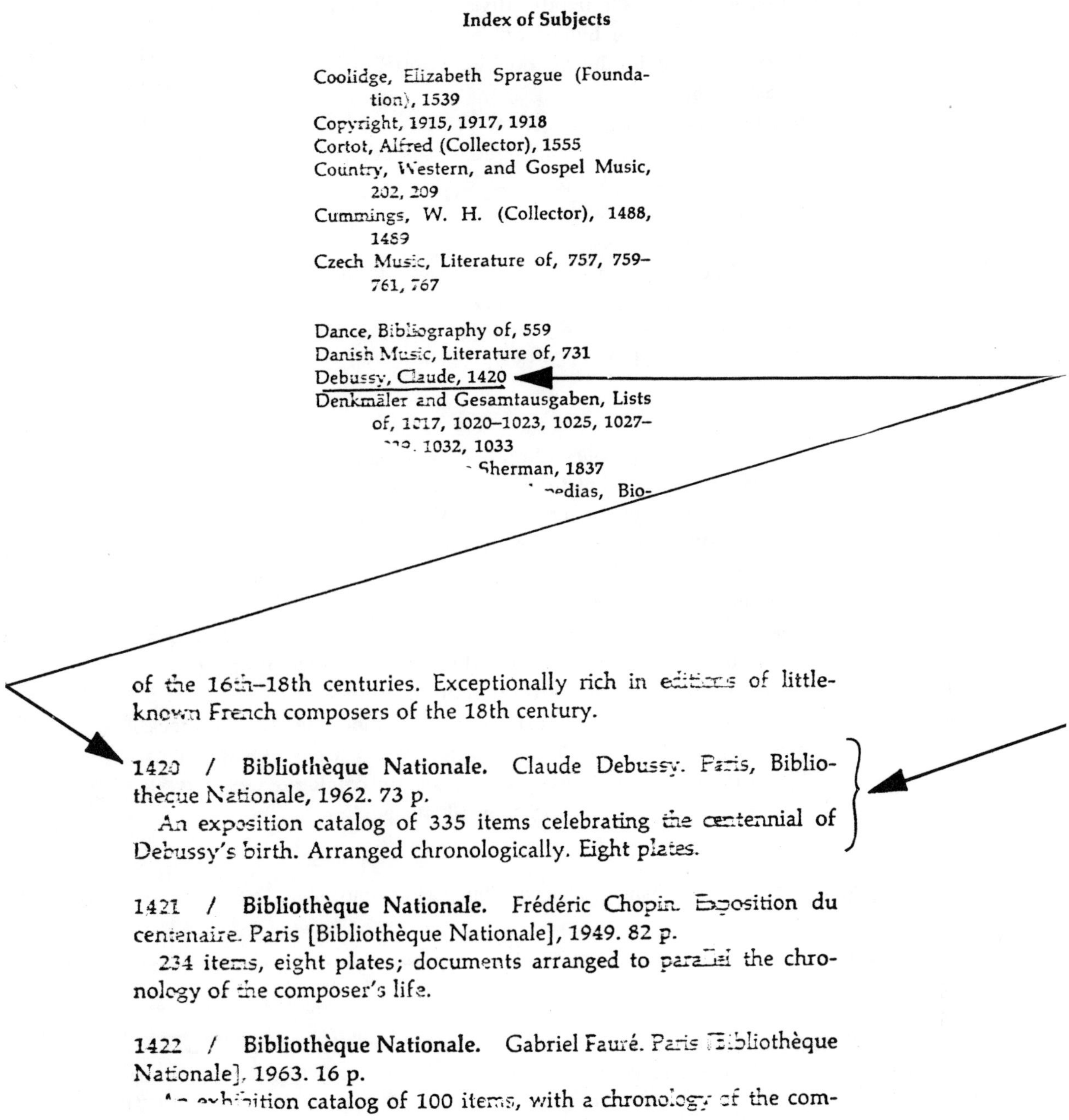

Coolidge, Elizabeth Sprague (Foundation), 1539
Copyright, 1915, 1917, 1918
Cortot, Alfred (Collector), 1555
Country, Western, and Gospel Music, 202, 209
Cummings, W. H. (Collector), 1488, 1489
Czech Music, Literature of, 757, 759–761, 767

Dance, Bibliography of, 559
Danish Music, Literature of, 731
Debussy, Claude, 1420
Denkmäler and Gesamtausgaben, Lists of, 1017, 1020–1023, 1025, 1027–1029, 1032, 1033
Sherman, 1837
dias, Bio-

of the 16th–18th centuries. Exceptionally rich in editions of little-known French composers of the 18th century.

1420 / **Bibliothèque Nationale.** Claude Debussy. Paris, Bibliothèque Nationale, 1962. 73 p.
An exposition catalog of 335 items celebrating the centennial of Debussy's birth. Arranged chronologically. Eight plates.

1421 / **Bibliothèque Nationale.** Frédéric Chopin. Exposition du centenaire. Paris [Bibliothèque Nationale], 1949. 82 p.
234 items, eight plates; documents arranged to parallel the chronology of the composer's life.

1422 / **Bibliothèque Nationale.** Gabriel Fauré. Paris [Bibliothèque Nationale], 1963. 16 p.
An exhibition catalog of 100 items, with a chronology of the com-

Figure 18. Duckles, Vincent. Music Reference and Research Materials. 3d ed. New York: The Free Press, 1974.

RILM, and the index entries, which at first glance seem rather frightening in their complexity, are actually loaded with useful information. As you can see in FIGURE 20, the cumulative index for volumes I–V (1967--71) gives an index reference under "Debussy . . . style" and also under "Stravinsky . . . style" which is pertinent to your topic. This reference shows the year of the citation (1970), the citation

number within that year (819), the source of the citation ("ap" stands for an article in a periodical), and the RILM classification (the number 28 refers to "Twentieth century, history"). The article cited appears in the periodical *Mens en Melodie* and is in Dutch, as you can learn by looking up "*MensMelodie*" and "Nl" in the list of abbreviations. Because of its systematic indexing and wide coverage, RILM

— Torri (Luigi). Del terzo Centenario della morte di Giovanni Croce detto il Chiozzotto (Rivista musicale italiana, XVI, 1909, pp. 550-562. Avec bibliographie).

**Curti.** Verzeichniss der Werke von Franz Curti. Loeschwitz, Curti, 1898, in-8, 8 p.

**Dancla.** Dancla (Charles). Notes et Souvenirs, 2ᵉ édition, revue et augmentée, suivie du catalogue de ses compositions. Paris, Bornemann, 1898, in-8, 175 p.

**Debussy.** Voyez I. Seré.

**Delibes.** Voyez I. Seré.

**Dittersdorf.** Kreus (Carl). Dittersdorfiana. Berlin, Paetel, 1900, in-8, vi-182 p. (Catalogue, pp. 55-144).

**Donizetti.** |Catalogo generale della mostra Donizettiana in Bergamo, '-' 99 VIII. al 22. IX, 1897. Parte I. Bergamo, Istituto d'arti

........

Schwan (Eduard). Die altfranzosischen ........ Verhältniss, ihre Entstehung und ihre Bestimmung. Eine literarhistorische Untersuchung. Berlin, Weidmann, 1886. in-8, 275 p.

Seiffert (Max). Die Chorbibliothek der Sanct-Michaelisschule in Lüneburg zu Seb. Bach's Zeit (Sammelbände der Internationalen Musikgesellschaft, IX, 1907-1909, pp. 593-621).

Seré (Octave). Musiciens français d'aujourd'hui, notices biographiques suivies d'un essai de bibliographie et accompagnées d'un autographe musical. Paris, Mercure de France, 1911, in-12, 416 p.

Servières (Georges). La musique française moderne. César Franck. Édouard Lalo. Jules Massenet. Ernest Reyer. Camille Saint-Saëns. Édition ornée de 5 portraits et suivie du catalogue des œuvres. Paris, Havard, 2ᵉ édit., 1896, in-16, 405 p., 5 portr.

Figure 19. Bobillier, Marie. "Bibliographie des bibliographies musicales." New York: De Capo, 1971.

---

is indispensable for finding material published since 1967.

Another important source for music literature — books as well as periodicals — is the *Bibliographie des Musikschrifttums (Bibliography of Writings on Music)* (Leipzig, Frankfurt am Main: Hofmeister, 1936– ). Publication began in 1936 but was suspended during the 1940s. Biennial volumes were issued for the period of the 1950s and annual ones have appeared since 1960. Unfortunately, publication dates lag far behind the volume dates. The volume for 1970, for example, did not appear until 1976.

This bibliography is international in coverage and is classified according to a hierarchy of main topics and subtopics not unlike that of RILM. Books, parts of books (including essays in *Festschriften* and other commemorative writings), and journals are all indexed. In the volume for 1970, about 340 titles (musical as well as non-musical) are listed in the index of periodicals and other source materials

("*Zeitschriften und Quellenverzeichnis*").

It is easy to trace the writings on Debussy and Stravinsky through the biographical ("*Personen*") section of each volume. The one for 1967, for example, cites a short article by Jeremy Noble: "Debussy and Stravinsky," *The Musical Times*, vol. 108 (1967), pp. 22–25. As you can see in FIGURE 21, this article appears under the heading "Debussy, Claude."

### Old Friends

You already have a bibliography card on the Noble article tucked away in your card file, since you found it earlier in the Debussy article in *The New Grove*. It also appeared in the 1967 volume of *The Music Index*, an important tool discussed in the last chapter. FIGURE 22 shows the ci-

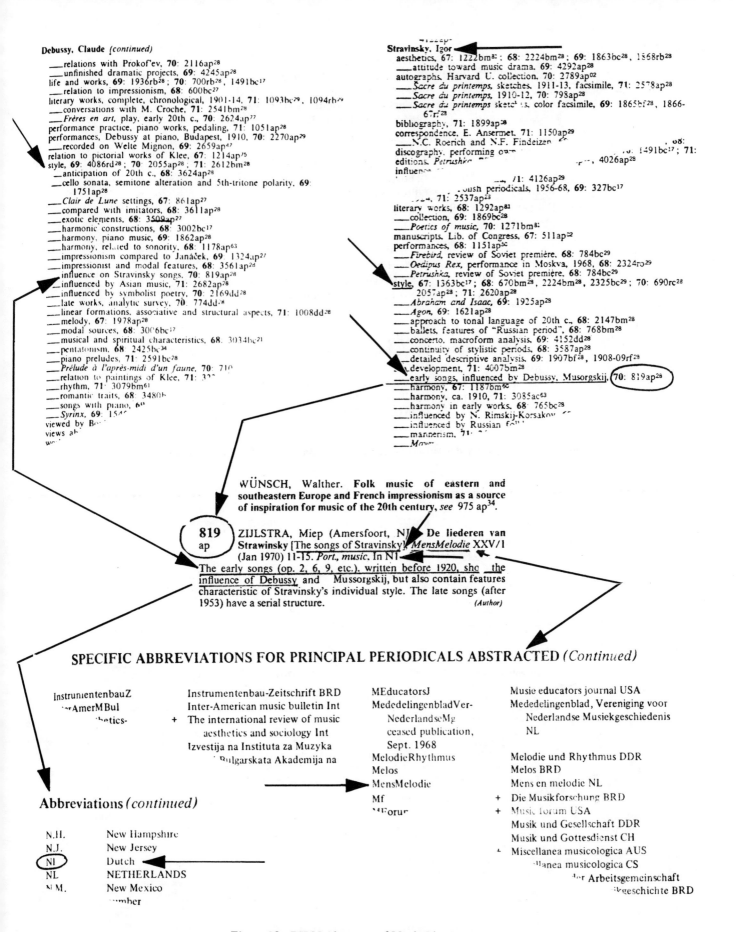

Figure 20. RILM Abstracts of Music Literature.

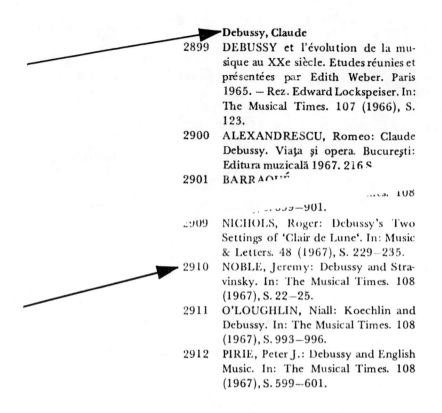

**Debussy, Claude**

2899  DEBUSSY et l'évolution de la musique au XXe siècle. Etudes réunies et présentées par Edith Weber. Paris 1965. — Rez. Edward Lockspeiser. In: The Musical Times. 107 (1966), S. 123.

2900  ALEXANDRESCU, Romeo: Claude Debussy. Viaţa şi opera. Bucureşti: Editura muzicală 1967. 216 S

2901  BARRAQUÉ

.....s. 108

... ...99—901.

2909  NICHOLS, Roger: Debussy's Two Settings of 'Clair de Lune'. In: Music & Letters. 48 (1967), S. 229—235.

2910  NOBLE, Jeremy: Debussy and Stravinsky. In: The Musical Times. 108 (1967), S. 22—25.

2911  O'LOUGHLIN, Niall: Koechlin and Debussy. In: The Musical Times. 108 (1967), S. 993—996.

2912  PIRIE, Peter J.: Debussy and English Music. In: The Musical Times. 108 (1967), S. 599—601.

Figure 21.  Bibliographie des Musikschrifttums.  Permission from B. Schott's Söhne, Mainz.

---

DEBUSSY, CLAUDE

After Webern, Wagner--reflections on the past and future of P.erre Boulez.  A. Whittall.  MUS R 28:135-8 n2 1967

Avant-premiere: Edgar Varese.  F. Ouellette.  port  J MUS FRANCAIS n153:38-40 Jan 1967

Claude Debussy in Selbstzeugnissen und Bilddokumenten.  J. Barraque.  See Barraque under BOOK REVIEWS

Claude Debussy und die Fünf.  A. Liess.  il  NEUE ZFM 128:69-77 Feb 1967

Debussy and Bartok.  A. Cross.  il  MUS T 108:125-7+ Feb 1967

Debussy and English music.  P. J. Pirie.  port  MUS T 108:599-601 Jul 1967

Debussy and French music.  R. Myers.  MUS T 108:899-901 Oct 1967

Debussy and Puccini.  M. Carner.  il  MUS T 108:502-5 Jun 1967

Debussy and Schoenberg.  R. Henderson.  MUS T 108:222-6 Mar 1967

[Debussy and Schoenberg.  R. Henderson] Letters to the editor: Berg and Debussy.  H. F. Redlich.  MUS T 108:428-9 May 1967

Debussy and Stravinsky.  J. Noble.  port  MUS T 108:22-5 Jan 1967

Debussy et l'evolution de la musique au XXe siecle.  Ed. by E. Weber.  See Weber under BOOK REVIEWS

Debussy: his life and mind.  Vol. 2: 1902-1918.  E. Lockspeiser.  See Lockspeiser under BOOK REVIEWS

The influence of Franck, Wagner, and Debussy on representative works of Ernest Chausson.  R. S. Grover.  DIS ABST 27:3072A-3A Mar 1967

Koechlin and Debussy.  N. O'Loughlin.  MUS T 108:993-6 Nov 1967

Nadar's 'pantheon.'  F. V. Grunfeld.  port  OPERA N 30:30 Feb 26 1966

Two pleas for a French, French music.  D. Bancroft.  MUS & LET 48:109-19 n2;  251-8 n3 1967

General Works

Aspetti tecnici e sviluppo storico del sistema 'esacordale' da Debussy in poi.  R. Dionisi.  il  R ITAL MUS 1:49-67 n1 1966

Interrelationship of impressionism and symbolism.  A. G. Duschak.  NATS 24:18-21 n1 1967

Where Ravel ends and Debussy begins.  C. Rosen.  port  (Reprinted from High Fidelity) 6:14-17 n9 1967

Works  [Clair de lune] Debussy's two settings of "Clair de Lune."  R

[Douze preludes, Book I, No. 10 (La cathedrale en
        CLAVIER 6:13-25 n9 1967

    [L'enfant prodigue] San Fr

    [Le martyre de

Figure 22.  The Music Index

tation from that volume. In the course of your work, some titles will appear again and again. They may even become "old friends." If this happens, do not feel that your search is being carried to excess. For most topics, many sources must be consulted — it is impossible to specify a minimum or maximum number — in order for the bibliographical ground to be covered with a reasonable degree of thoroughness. It is inevitable that some books and articles will be cited in more than one source.

### Bibliographies of Music

The field of bibliographies of music — that is, music scores as opposed to writings about music — is so vast that only the briefest of surveys can be offered here. For your purposes, since you are dealing with a term paper on Debussy and Stravinsky, general bibliographies of music will probably be of limited assistance. And bibliographies which deal with early music, though exceptionally important to the field of music history as a whole, need be mentioned only in passing.

The most comprehensive and important of the bibliographies of early music is the *International Inventory of Musical Sources*, widely known by its acronym "RISM," for *Répertoire internationale des sources musicales* (München-Duisburg: G. Henle, 1960– ). It is the objective of RISM, which is still in progress (more than twenty volumes have been published thus far), to cover all known printed publications and manuscripts of music which appeared before about 1800. (Strictly speaking, this invaluable work belongs in the category of bibliographies which list both music and music literature, since writings on music theory are included.)

Two important predecessors of RISM were both compiled single-handedly by a nineteenth-century bibliographer well-known to music historians, Robert Eitner (1832–1905). The first, his *Bibliographie der Musik-Sammelwerke des XVI. und XVII. Jahrhunderts (Bibliography of Music Collections of the Sixteenth and Seventeenth Centuries)* (Berlin: L. Liepmannssohn, 1877) lists the contents of hundreds of collections (i.e., anthologies) published between 1501 and 1700. The second, and more important, is his *Biographisch-bibliographisches Quellen-Lexikon der Musiker und Musikgelehrten der christlichen Zeitrechnung bis zur Mitte des 19. Jahrhunderts (Biographical-bibliographical Source-lexicon of Musicians and Music Scholars from the Early Christian Era to the Middle of the Nineteenth Century)* (Leipzig: Breitkopf & Härtel, 1900–1904), a ten-volume work often referred to simply as the *"Quellen-Lexikon."* It is a publication of immense labor and scope which gives biographical information and the European library source for the publications and manuscripts listed.

You may find that one of the more difficult tasks in music research — though sometimes only frustrating rather than intellectually difficult — is to locate a particular composition which may be in a collection, anthology, or publisher's series, and does not appear separately in the card catalog. The search for songs in collections is aided by the following tools: Minnie Earl Sears, *Song Index: An Index to More than 12000 Songs in 177 Song Collections . . .* (New York: H.W. Wilson, 1926); and the same author's *Song Index Supplement: An Index to More Than 7000 Songs in 104 Song Collections . . .* (New York, H.W. Wilson, 1934); and Desiree de Charms and Paul F. Breed, *Songs in Collections: An Index* (Detroit: Information Service Incorp., 1966). The Sears volumes, even though published decades ago, are still useful. The De Charms and Breed index covers 411 collections published from about 1940 to 1957; its listing of almost 9,500 songs thus supplements Sears.

The basic volume by Sears lists eleven songs by Debussy (p. 127) and one by Stravinsky (p. 536). This last song, identified as "The Cloister" here, is traced in FIGURE 23 from the composer entry to the title entry, where the anthology symbol appears, and then on to the "key to symbols" sec-

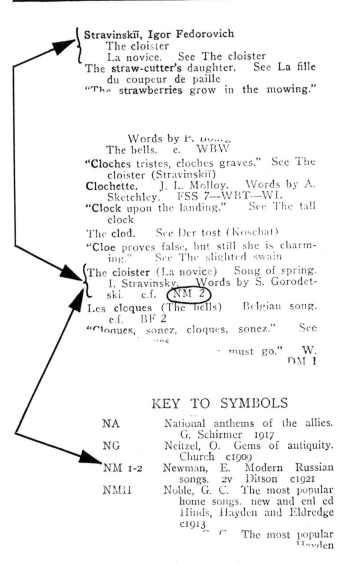

**Figure 23. Sears, Minnie Earl. Song Index. New York: H.W. Wilson, 1926.**

tion. Sears' supplementary volume lists two additional songs by Debussy (p. 67) and none by Stravinsky. The two composers fare slightly better in the index by De Charms and Breed: Debussy has fifteen songs listed (pp. 28--29) and Stravinsky two (p. 128). The sources of these last two songs are traced in FIGURE 24. (Of course it must be recognized that because of copyright restrictions, the works of twentieth-

century composers — Debussy and Stravinsky in particular — are less likely to appear in miscellaneous collections and anthologies than the works of earlier composers which are in the public domain.)

Happily, the three Stravinsky songs located by means of these indexes are clearly pertinent to your topic. They are identified as *Pastorale* (1907) and *Two Melodies*, op. 6 (1907–

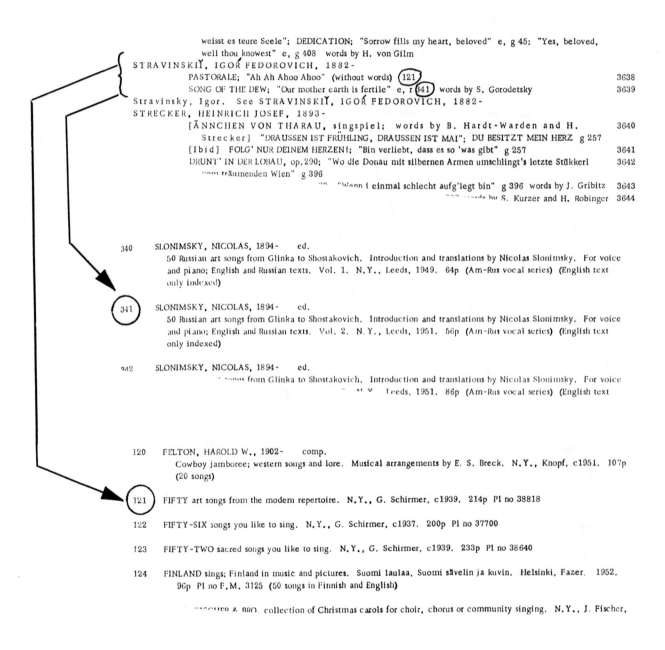

Figure 24. De Charms, Desiree, and Breed, Paul F. Songs in Collections. Detroit: Information Service Incorporated, 1966.

08) in E.W. White's *Stravinsky: The Composer and His Works*, 2d ed., mentioned previously (see White, pp. 177–179). You will recall from the RILM abstract shown in FIGURE 20 that the songs written before 1920 are considered to have been influenced by Debussy.

Only a few other reference tools are similar in function to the song indexes just described. For major music collections (vocal as well as instrumental) and composer editions, the primary tool is Anna Harriet Heyer, *Historical Sets, Collected Editions, and Monuments of Music: A Guide to Their Contents*, 2d ed. (Chicago: American Library Association, 1969). Though rapidly becoming outdated — the cut-off date for inclusion of material was spring, 1966 — Heyer remains the most comprehensive and detailed index of its kind. The contents of more than 900 publications are listed; a composer index (with a small number of subjects included) provides references to the main publication entry. For example, Stravinsky appears in the index by virtue of an organ transcription (of an excerpt from his ballet, *L'Oiseau de feu*), which was included in a historical anthology of solo organ pieces. As FIGURE 25 illustrates, the index must be used to trace the anthology which contains this transcription.

Supplementing Heyer (but not updating it by much more than two years, for the most part) is Sydney Robinson Charles, *A Handbook of Music and Music Literature in Sets and Series* (New York: The Free Press, 1972), a versatile resource which will be discussed below, under bibliographies which cover both music and music literature.

## Music Publications Available for Purchase

Books currently available from bookstores, distributors, or publishers are considered "in print." If no longer available, they are, as you might suspect, "out of print" ("OP" in library terminology). There is at present no single compilation which brings together all domestically published music in print as do the following for books: *Books in Print* (New York: R.R. Bowker, 1948– ) and its related publication, *Subject Guide to Books in Print* (New York: R.R. Bowker, 1957– ). There is, however, a "Music-in-Print" series currently underway, and it includes both foreign and domestic publications. Under the editorship of Thomas R. Nardone (and others) and published by Musicdata, Inc. (Philadelphia), the series has progressed thus far to date:

*Sacred Choral Music in Print* (1974)
*Secular Choral Music in Print* (1974)
*Choral Music in Print: 1976 Supplement*
*Organ Music in Print* (1975)
*Classical Vocal Music in Print* (1976)
*Orchestral Music in Print* (1979)

To take one of these volumes as an example, in *Classical Vocal Music in Print*, composers, titles, and cross references are interfiled in one alphabet, with the composer entry being the main one unless a work is anonymous, in which case the title entry is the main one. In the case of vocal anthologies

containing no more than six pieces, each piece is individually indexed. Debussy is represented here by nearly 100 separate publications (pp. 122–123) containing his solo vocal music (including songs as well as operatic arias and excerpts from other vocal works) — a substantial part of his entire solo vocal output. Stravinsky, not so prolific in this area as Debussy, is represented by about twenty publications (p. 555).

Other "in-print" publications include the following: Margaret K. Farish, *String Music in Print*, 2d ed. (New York: R.R. Bowker, 1973); and Joseph Rezits and Gerald Deatsman, *The Pianist's Resource Guide: Piano Music in Print and Literature on the Pianistic Art*, 2d ed. (Park Ridge, IL:

INDEX

?In: Thouret. Musik am preussischen Hofe. No.20.
Three valses.
In: Denkmäler der Tonkunst in Österreich. Vol.63. (Jg.XXXII/2).
STRAUSS, JOSEF, 1827–1870.
Three valses.
In: Denkmäler der Tonkunst in Österreich. Vol.74. (Jg.XXXVIII/2).
STRAUSS, RICHARD, 1864–1949.
Lieder. 4v.
STRAVINSKIĬ, IGOR' FEDOROVICH. 1882– .
Rondo des Princesses (From "The fire bird"). Organ.
In: Dickinson. Historical recital series for organ. Vol.1. No.2.
STRIGGIO, ALESSANDRO. ca.1535–a.1587.
Selections.
In: Documenta historica musicae.
In: Torchi. L'arte musicale in Italia. Bd.1.
Il cicalamento delle Donne al Bucato.
Capolavori polifonici del secolo

Das deutsche Lied. *see* Reimann, Heinrich. Das deutsche Lied.

DICKINSON, CLARENCE, 1873– . ed.
Historical recital series for organ, ed. and arr. by Clarence Dickinson. New York, H. W. Gray Co., Inc., [cop.1917–cop.1920].
2v. and 8 nos.
Each number is also published separately.
Contents:
Vol.1.
No.1. Stamitz, K. Andante.
No.2. Stravinsky, I. Rondo des princesses (From "The fire bird").
No.3. Quantz, J. J. Arioso (Sonata 333).
No.4. Quantz, J. J. Presto (Sonata 333).
No.5. Rousseau, J. J. Minuet (From Le devin

**Figure 25. Reprinted by permission of the American Library Association from Historical Sets, Collected Editions, and Monuments of Music, by Anna Harriet Heyer, copyright (c) 1969 by the American Library Association.**

Pallma Music Co., 1978).

## Bibliographies Covering both Music and Music Literature

In the area of bibliographies which cover both music and music literature, library catalogs comprise an important subgroup. First and foremost are those issued by the Library of Congress (frequently referred to here as "LC"). The publication history of the LC catalogs, which have been issued in various series since 1942, is somewhat complicated and need not be described in detail here. The most important titles to remember are the following: *The National Union Catalog: Pre-1956 Imprints* (London: Mansell, 1968– ) and *National Union Catalog* (Washington, DC: Library of Congress, 1956– ). These works cover various works concerning the literature of music. The former, which includes only books and music scores published before 1956, is a catalog of monumental proportions. It will reach some 700 or more volumes (comprising some 10 million entires) when completed, thus making it beyond all doubt the largest bibliography ever compiled. The latter includes, as a continuing supplement, *Music and Phonorecords*, whose title was changed in 1973 to *Music, Books on Music, and Sound Recordings*. All along, this supplement had embraced music scores, sheet music, libretti, and sound recordings (both musical and nonmusical), and the title was altered to reflect its scope more accurately.

FIGURE 26 shows the entries for Debussy's *En blanc et noir* in volume 136 of *The National Union Catalog: Pre-1956 Imprints*. This is but a minute section of the space devoted to Debussy — there are by rough estimate over 1,000 entries under Debussy in this volume (pp. 148–192).

Taken together, these National Union Catalogs presently embody the combined contributions, in the form of separate catalog entries, of 700 or more libraries in the United States and Canada, including the Library of Congress. If you need bibliographical data or the library location for even the most obscure titles, these catalogs can often be helpful.

Another useful Library of Congress series is the following: U.S. Library of Congress, *Library of Congress Catalog – Books: Subjects* . . . (Washington, DC: Library of Congress, 1950– ). Included are titles cataloged by the Library of Congress and arranged according to the LC subject headings which have been assigned. Thus you will find books (but not music) under subject headings such as DEBUSSY, CLAUDE, 1862–1918; STRAVINSKIĬ, IGOR' FEDERO-VICH, 1882–1971 (in 1981 the authorized form of the name was changed to STRAVINSKY, IGOR); and IMPRESSION-ISM (MUSIC). Headings related to music in France, for example, MUSIC – FRANCE – HISTORY AND CRITICISM, will also be found. (Strictly speaking, this LC series belongs in the section above devoted to bibliographies of music literature but was included here because of its close relationship with the other LC catalogs.)

The LC catalogs, since they are indispensable for cata-

loging, may be available only in the cataloging department of your library. If so, ask your reference librarian or your catalog librarian to point them out. You will have no trouble in gaining access to these important publications, because librarians, in most instances, are happy to see interest on the part of the library patron in the librarian's "tools of the trade."

Next to the Library of Congress, the New York Public Library has this country's largest collection of music and music literature. The published catalog of this collection is therefore of no small importance: The New York Public Library, Reference Department, *Dictionary Catalog of the Music Collection* (Boston: G.K. Hall, 1964–65; 33 vols.; *Supplement 1*, 1966; *Cumulative Supplement, 1964–1971*, 10 vols., 1973). Similar to the LC catalogs, this one and its supplements consist of photographic reproductions of catalog cards. Author and subject entries for both books and scores (and, in the basic set, even journal articles) are interfiled in one alphabetical arrangement. Some subject headings (and some aspects of the filing arrangement also) differ somewhat from LC practice. For example, volume 9, page 56, of the basic set displays an entry with the heading DEBUSSY, CLAUDE – STRAVINSKI, as shown in FIGURE 27. No such combination of personal name headings is admissible according to LC subject heading practice. But, luckily, here you find an article which should prove useful:

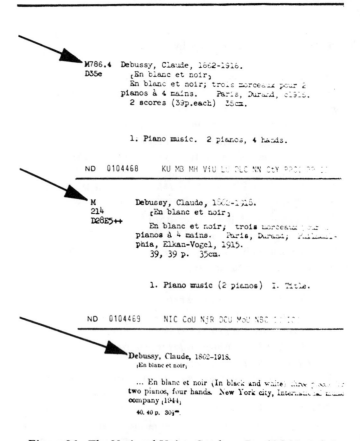

**Figure 26. The National Union Catalog: Pre 1956 Imprints.**

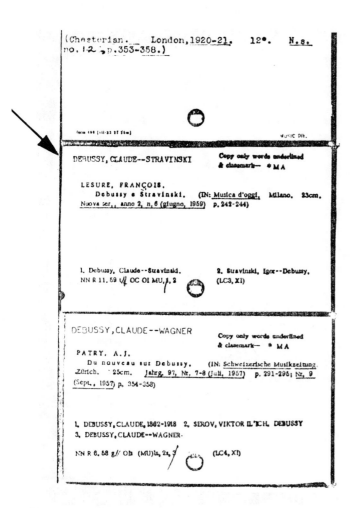

(Chesterian. London,1920-21. 12°. N.s. no. 1-2, p.353-358.)

DEBUSSY, CLAUDE--STRAVINSKI

Copy only words underlined & classmark-- * M A

LESURE, FRANÇOIS.
Debussy e Stravinski. (IN: Musica d'oggi, Milano. 23cm. Nuova ser., anno 2, n. 6 (giugno, 1959) p. 242-244)

1. Debussy, Claude--Stravinski.
NN R 11. 59 v/ OC OI MU, J. 2

2. Stravinski, Igor--Debussy.
(LC3, XI)

DEBUSSY, CLAUDE--WAGNER

Copy only words underlined & classmark-- * M A

PATRY, A. J.
Du nouveau sur Debussy. (IN: Schweizerische Musikzeitung. Zürich. 25cm. Jahrg. 97, Nr. 7-8 (Juli, 1957) p. 291-295; Nr. 9 (Sept., 1957) p. 354-358)

1. DEBUSSY, CLAUDE, 1862-1918 2. SEROV, VIKTOR IL'ICH. DEBUSSY 3. DEBUSSY, CLAUDE--WAGNER.
NN R 6. 58 g// Ob (MU)k, 2t,
(LC4, XI)

**Figure 27. Dictionary Catalog of the Music Collection, New York Public Library.**

François Lesure, "Debussy e Stravinsky," *Musica d'Oggi*, vol. 2 (June, 1959), pp. 242–244. (Once again you are confronted with a foreign language reference — this time in Italian. But even if you do not read Italian, this article should not be set aside, since it is obviously of direct interest to your topic. Recall the discussion on foreign language skills in the section, "Measuring the depth of your topic," in Chapter 2.)

Further supplementing the New York Public Library music catalog is a series of annual bibliographies which began publication soon after the New York Public Library cumulative supplement (1964–71) appeared: *Bibliographic Guide to Music: 1975--* (Boston: G.K. Hall, 1976– ). Here, catalog entries supplied by The Research Libraries of the New York Public Library are interfiled with entries from MARC (*MA*chine *R*eadable *C*ataloging) computer tapes supplied by the Library of Congress. While not as complete by far as an "in-print" publication or a current national bibliography, such as the *American Book Publishing Record* (New York:

R.R. Bowker, 1960– ), these bibliographies provide a fair representation of recently published music and music literature; the bibliographical detail given in the catalog entries is in accordance with LC standards, and subject headings and cross references conform to the LC subject heading guide. Thorough cross-indexing makes it easy to look up the publications concerning either Debussy or Stravinsky.

Coming back to *A Handbook of Music and Music Literature in Sets and Series,* by Sydney Robinson Charles, we find that it includes many fewer music editions than another title already discussed, Heyer's *Historical Sets, Collected Editions, and Monuments of Music.* Charles cites 197 music editions, as opposed to the 900 in Heyer. In addition, Charles provides illuminating details about sixty-one music periodicals and yearbooks. All but one of the references to Debussy and Stravinsky pertain to monographs and special issues of periodicals.

## The Computer

A truly remarkable supplement to the card catalog is the computer. It has facilitated the publication of a growing number of music bibliographies and indexes, among them: RILM, the Musicdata "in-print" publications, the G.K. Hall *Bibliographic Guides*, and the Rezits and Deatsman guide to piano publications (all mentioned in this chapter). The computer has also made possible the rise of bibliographic computer networks with astounding capabilities and a potential that seems unlimited. OCLC (now known as "OCLC Online Computer Library Center, Incorporated"), which began on-line operations (i.e., operations involving immediate interaction between a computer terminal and a data base, as opposed to off-line operations, in which data is first stored before being processed by the computer) at its Columbus, Ohio, headquarters in the fall of 1971, is now the largest of these networks. By typing in a particular sequence of letters or numbers on a special keyboard attached to a cathode ray terminal (CRT), a person at any one of the hundreds of OCLC member libraries may have displayed on the CRT the bibliographic data pertinent to one or more of the several million (!) catalog records presently in the system. The data base is continually enriched by cataloging information transmitted to OCLC headquarters by member libraries via the CRT, in addition to bibliographic records supplied by the Library of Congress through MARC tapes. In other words, the number of catalog records available keeps growing by leaps and bounds. FIGURE 28 shows a "print-out" (a permanent record of the information displayed on the CRT, obtained from a special printing machine attached to the CRT) of the Abravanel bibliography displayed at an OCLC terminal.

Another important bibliographic system, BALLOTS (for *B*ibliographic *A*utomation of *L*arge *L*ibrary *O*perations using a *T*ime-sharing *S*ystem), centered at the Stanford University Libraries at Stanford, California, is more versatile

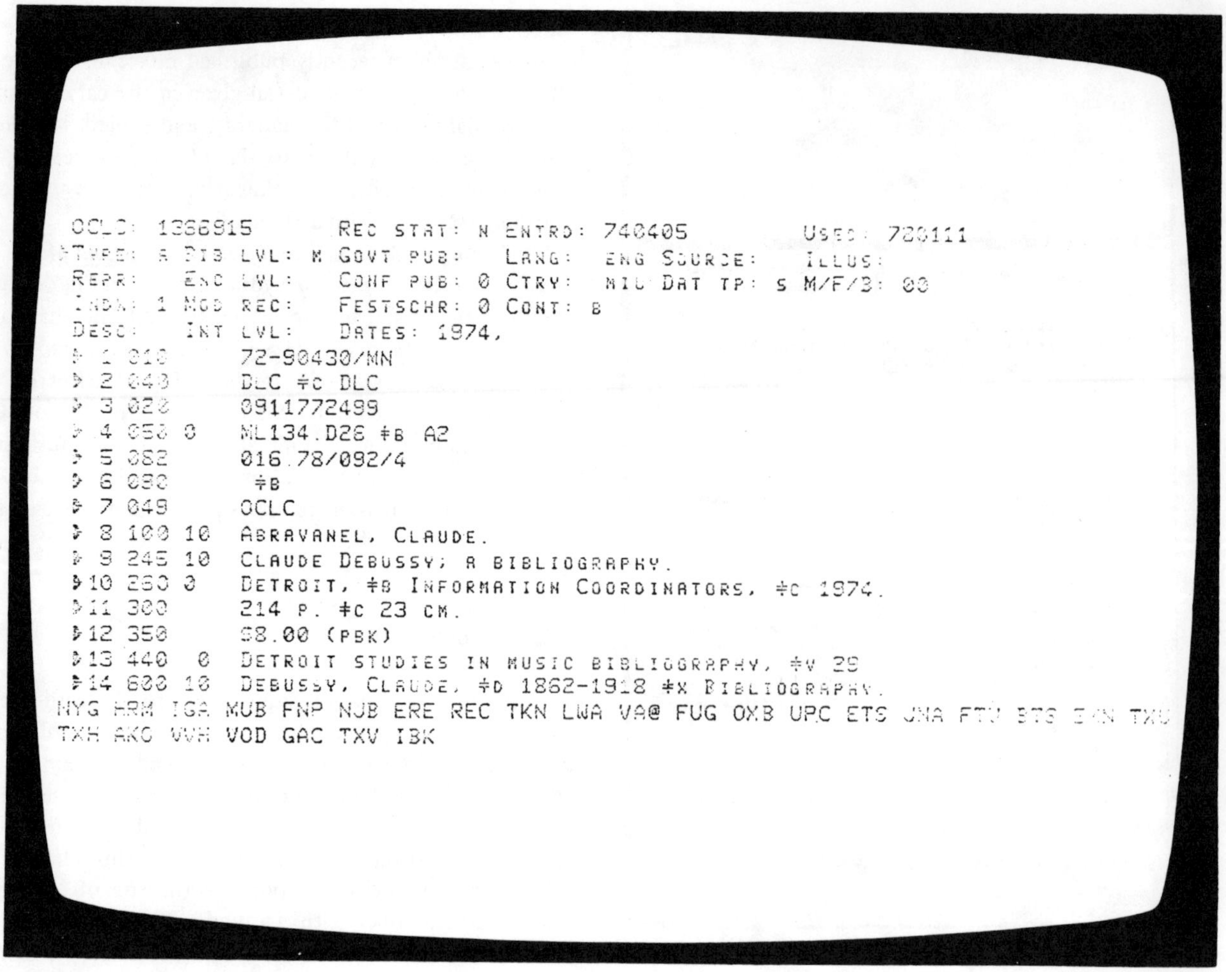

**Figure 28. Print-out from an OCLC terminal.**

than OCLC with regard to user interaction and data manipulation, but is smaller in terms of the data base, the number of member libraries, and their geographic distribution.

There has been widespread discussion about the possibility that the computer may someday replace the card catalog in many libraries. It certainly has the potential to do so. In some libraries, use of the computer has already superseded that of the card catalog for certain technical operations. If your library is a member of a bibliographic system, or has access to commercial data bases, ask your reference or catalog librarian about the opportunities for extending your search to the computer. You may be able to find materials that were unlisted in the various reference works previously consulted, and, just as importantly, you may have a glimpse of the search strategy of the future.

**Summary**

1. Do not succumb to the temptation to break off your search too early. A thorough search means looking into a wide variety of reference tools, including bibliographies and similar resources.

2. Just as Caesar's Gaul was divided into three parts, the bibliographical world of music can be divided into (a) bibliographies of music literature, (b) bibliographies of music, and (c) bibliographies covering both music literature and music. In this context, music literature is to be understood as writings on the subject of music, music as music scores.

3. Do not conclude that you are overdoing it if you find two or more references to the same book or article in the course of your search. Thorough coverage of the bibliographical literature often brings out repeated references to some materials.

4. There is no comprehensive "in-print" publication for music, but several tools cover a large portion of the vocal and instrumental scores currently available.

5. The computer is becoming a major tool for bibliographical research; opportunities for using the computer in your library should be investigated.

"The theme is sizable, clearly shaped and clean cut; it has its countenance, its character, its mood."
— Toch (from *The Shaping Forces in Music*)

## What Is a Thematic Index?

A thematic index or catalog (the two terms are usually used interchangeably) is a special type of music bibliography which covers the works of one composer, a group of composers, or in some cases one or more manuscripts or printed publications, and lists systematically the themes or incipits (beginnings) of works so that they may be readily identified. Individual thematic indexes for the major composers usually contain, along with each composition or group of compositions, a statement about the date of composition, date of publication, performance requirements (i.e., medium of performance and instrumentation), and other details. In some instances, bibliographies concerning individual works are provided. The standard terminology for the thematic index in German is *thematisches Verzeichnis*, in French, *catalogue thématique* (the term *catalogue raisonné* is reserved for the non-thematic catalog, which is discussed later in this chapter).

## Why Is It Useful?

The value of the thematic index is self-evident (well, almost). By glancing through some of the major ones — for example, those of J.S. Bach, Mozart, and Beethoven — you can see immediately that you have in a convenient format a substantial amount of bibliographical information about individual works.

You also have a means of identifying particular works. Have you ever wondered which Debussy *Prélude* it is whose theme comes back to haunt you? Or what information to provide in identifying works for a recital program? If so, a thematic index may be your best tool.

## The Definitive Publication

The definitive publication on this type of resource is Barry S. Brook, *Thematic Catalogues in Music: An Annotated Bibliography* (Hillsdale, NY: Pendragon, 1972). Brook identifies no fewer than 1,444 published and unpublished items which contain thematic indexes or include information about them. Debussy is represented by three separate entries (citation numbers 283, 283a, and 284), shown in FIGURE 29. Of these three, the English version of the Vallas biography (reprint, New York: Dover Publications, 1973) is the only one readily available at present. In an appendix of this biography, the incipits of 178 individually titled compositions (all published) by Debussy are provided. The entry for *En blanc et noir*, whose third movement you may recall was dedicated to Stravinsky, is shown in

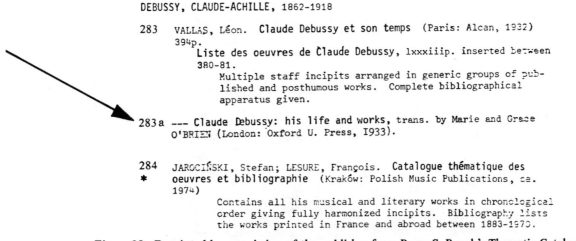

Figure 29. Reprinted by permission of the publisher from Barry S. Brook's Thematic Catalogues in Music, Pendragon Press, New York, 1972.

FIGURE 30.

Brook does not list Stravinsky as the subject of a separate thematic index, even though White's *Stravinsky: The Composer and His Works*, 2d ed., mentioned earlier, very nearly qualifies as this kind of tool. Part II ("Register of Works," pp. 161–551) describes systematically and in chronological order 109 original works plus arrangements of other composers' works. 201 musical excerpts and examples are interwoven into the text. The entries for some works lack musical examples, while others contain several.

## A Variety of Formats

Thematic catalogs which are intended exclusively as aids for identification purposes are likely to have a format radically different from those of the major composers. Of special significance for research in early music is John R. Bryden and David G. Hughes, *An Index of Gregorian Chant* (Cambridge, MA: Harvard University Press, 1969), a two-volume publication. We are dealing here with a large body of Gregorian melodies, many of them stemming from the early Christian era, and their texts. The objective is to be able to identify the melody or melodies that are associated with a particular text in the chant repertory, and vice versa. In volume 1 of this index, incipits of texts are listed in alphabetical order and paired with melodic incipits which are expressed in a special numerical notation designating melodic intervals. Abbreviations for the chant-book sources are given along with each pair. Volume 2 presents things the other way around: this time the melodic incipits are listed in a special numerical framework and paired with textual incipits. Thus it is not difficult to find a complete chant if you have either the text or the melody to work with. See, for example, the listings for the Gradual, *Haec dies quam fecit*, shown in FIGURE 31.

Figure 30. Vallas, Léon. Claude Debussy. New York: Dover Publications, 1973.

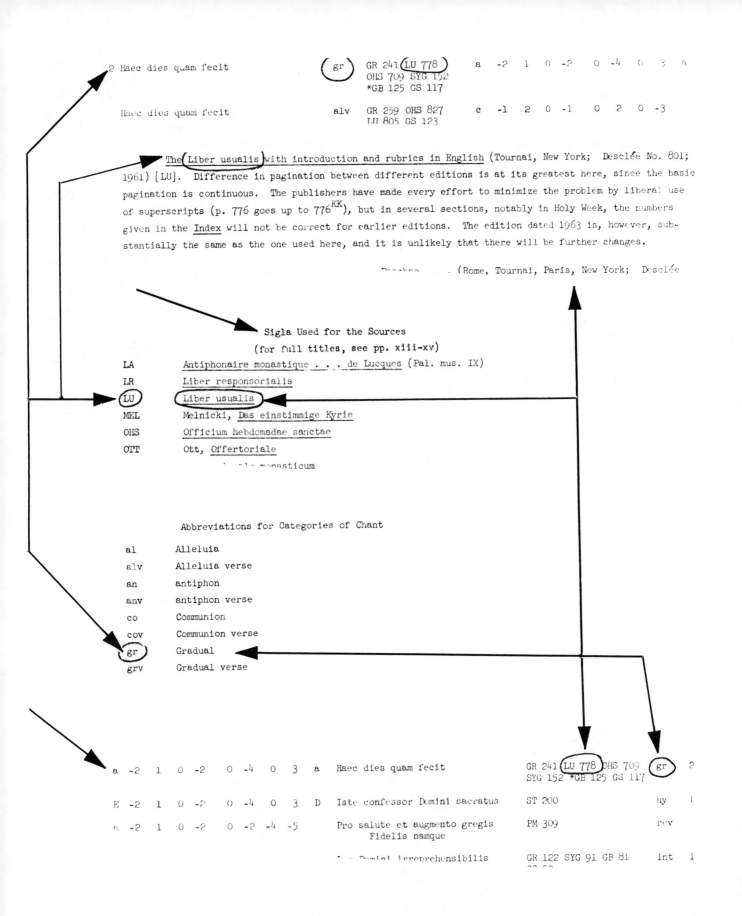

2 Haec dies quam fecit      (gr)   GR 241 (LU 778)
     OHS 709 SYG 152
     *GB 125 GS 117
     a   -2   1   0   -2   0   -4   0   3   a

Haec dies quam fecit      alv   GR 259 OHS 827
     LU 805 GS 123
     c   -1   2   0   -1   0   2   0   -3

The (Liber usualis) with introduction and rubrics in English (Tournai, New York; Desclée No. 801; 1961) [LU]. Difference in pagination between different editions is at its greatest here, since the basic pagination is continuous. The publishers have made every effort to minimize the problem by liberal use of superscripts (p. 776 goes up to $776^{KK}$), but in several sections, notably in Holy Week, the numbers given in the Index will not be correct for earlier editions. The edition dated 1963 is, however, substantially the same as the one used here, and it is unlikely that there will be further changes.

        ......... . (Rome, Tournai, Paris, New York; Desclée

### Sigla Used for the Sources
(for full titles, see pp. xiii-xv)

LA     Antiphonaire monastique . . . . de Lucques (Pal. mus. IX)
LR     Liber responsorialis
(LU)    Liber usualis
MEL    Melnicki, Das einstimmige Kyrie
OHS    Officium hebdomadae sanctae
OTT    Ott, Offertoriale
        ...... monasticum

### Abbreviations for Categories of Chant

al     Alleluia
alv    Alleluia verse
an     antiphon
anv    antiphon verse
co     Communion
cov    Communion verse
(gr)    Gradual
grv    Gradual verse

a   -2   1   0   -2   0   -4   0   3   a   Haec dies quam fecit     GR 241 (LU 778) OHS 709 (gr)   2
                                                   SYG 152 *GB 125 GS 117

E   -2   1   0   -2   0   -4   0   3   D   Iste confessor Domini sacratus     ST 200     hy   1

a   -2   1   0   -2   0   -2   -4   -5   Pro salute et augmento gregis     PM 309     rev
                                            Fidelis namque

                           ... Domini irreprehensibilis     GR 122 SYG 91 GB 81     int   1

**Figure 31. Bryden, John R. and Hughes, David G. An Index of Gregorian Chant. Cambridge, Mass: Harvard University Press, 1969.**

An alphabetic system of notation, designed to help you remember any of a large number of melodies from the so-called standard repertory, appears in Harold Barlow and Sam Morgenstern, *A Dictionary of Musical Themes* (New York: Crown, 1948) and, by the same authors, *A Dictionary of Opera and Song Themes, Including Cantatas, Oratorios, Lieder, and Art Songs* (New York: Crown, 1966).

## The Non-Thematic Catalog, or "Catalogue Raisonné"

Resources which contain systematically arranged bibliographical information about the works of one or more composers, but which lack thematic incipits or excerpts, as in the case of the *catalogue raisonné*, are not uncommon. Sometimes they supplement a particular thematic index with additional indexes and cross references. In the case of Stravinsky, the following guide offers an alphabetical bibliography of works and arrangements, indexed by publisher, medium of performance, names of individuals and groups associated with one or more works (as performers, poets, and so forth), and a chronological index of works: Dominique-René de Lerma, *Igor Fedorovitch Stravinsky; A Practical Guide to Publications of His Music* (Kent, OH: Kent State University Press, 1974). Debussy is easily identified here in the name index (p. 137) as one to whom Stravinsky dedicated one or more works.

A *catalogue raisonné* issued by the publisher Durand on the occasion of the centennial anniversary of Debussy's birth is entitled *Catalogue de l'oeuvre de Claude Debussy (Catalog of the Works of Claude Debussy)* (Paris: Durand, 1962). Significantly, it includes a rather sizable list of works that were projected, left incomplete, or unpublished (see pp. 107–108). A catalog of the same kind, but considerably more detailed and more recent, is François Lesure, *Catalogue de l'oeuvre de Claude Debussy* (Genève: Éditions Minkoff, 1977), which lists, in chronological order, 141 works, plus various other ephemeral or fragmentary compositions. This publication, like the Abravanel bibliography, is a "must" for Debussy scholars. FIGURE 32 shows the entry for *En blanc et noir*.

---

134

### EN BLANC ET NOIR

*Trois morceaux pour 2 pianos à 4 mains*

I. [Épigraphe :] Qui reste à sa place
Et ne danse pas
De quelque disgrâce
Fait l'aveu tout bas.

(J. Barbier & M. Carré, *Roméo et Juliette*)

II.  Prince, porté soit des serfs Eolus
En la forest ou domine Glaucus
Ou privé soit de paix et d'espérance
Car digne n'est de posséder vertus
Qui mal vouldroit au royaume de France.

(F. Villon, *Ballade contre les ennemis de la France*)

III.  Yver, vous n'estes qu'un vilain.

(Charles d'Orléans)

Date : 4 juin-20 juillet 1915.

Ms. autographe : Bibliothèque nationale, Ms. 989 (22 pages) ; un autre manuscrit comportant des corrections au crayon par l'auteur a passé en vente à l'Hôtel Drouot Cornuau) le 16 novembre 1935 (32 pages).

Dédicataires : A. Kussewitsky (I), Jacques Charlot (II), Igor Stravinsky (III).

Édition : Durand, 1915 ; Leipzig, Peters, 1973 (par E. Klemm).

1re audition : le 21 décembre 1916, par Debussy et Roger Ducasse, chez Mme Georges Guiard (matinée au profit du « Vêtement du prisonnier de guerre »).

Commentaire : les dates précises de composition indiquées ci-dessus sont extraites d'un agenda de travail ayant appartenu à Debussy (Bibliothèque nationale).
Le titre devait être originellement « Caprices en blanc et noir ».
Le 2 décembre 1915, Debussy déchiffrait l'œuvre sur épreuves avec Louis Aubert, chez Durand.

Bibliographie : L. Vallas, p. 407 ; Dietschy, p. 232.

Figure 32. Lesure, François. Catalogue de l'oeuvre de Claude Debussy. Genève: Éditions Minkoff, 1977.

### A Postscript

In your library, thematic indexes or catalogs will be identified in the card catalog under the name of the composer, with the subject heading subdivision — THEMATIC CATALOGS. If you discover a particular need for one that does not exist, you may eventually decide to prepare it yourself. Your efforts are bound to be rewarded if you follow the example of one of the many fine publications of this type currently available.

### Summary

1. Thematic indexes or catalogs are useful because, for the most part, they provide systematically arranged bibliographical information and also a musical means of identifying particular works.
2. The formats of thematic indexes vary widely; those intended exclusively for purposes of identifying melodies sometimes employ numeric or alphabetic notation.
3. The non-thematic catalog, or *catalogue raisonné*, sometimes contains useful information which supplements a related thematic catalog.

## Registers and Abstracts

Since 1951, music students engaged in research — graduate students in particular — have consulted various editions of *Doctoral Dissertations in Musicology* (5th ed.; Philadelphia: American Musicological Society, 1971), along with supplements published in the *Journal of the American Musicological Society* (1948– ). Dissertations from universities in the United States and Canada only are listed here. Succeeding *Doctoral Dissertations in Musicology* and incorporating many foreign dissertations is Cecil Adkins and Alis Dickinson, eds., *International Index of Doctoral Dissertations and Musicological Works in Progress* (Philadelphia: American Musicological Society, 1977). It lists no fewer than 4,641 titles, more than twice the number in the fifth edition of *Doctoral Dissertations in Musicology*. A supplement was published in 1979.

The Adkins and Dickinson index is a major contribution to the bibliography of music. It is important because it provides a comprehensive list of dissertations and other musicological works which were complete or in progress as of 1979. You may be aware that there is a great need to keep the scholarly community — students, teachers, and other researchers alike — aware of the current state of research so that duplication of effort can be avoided as much as possible. In fact, in most universities and graduate divisions, a dissertation topic which falls closely along the lines of one previously listed in Adkins and Dickinson is not likely to be approved.

Adkins and Dickinson can also be used to some extent as an "in-print" list, since many of the completed dissertations are commercially available in photocopy or microfilm format. Most of those from universities in the United States and Canada can be obtained from Xerox University Microfilms in Ann Arbor, Michigan. It is important to keep this point in mind because few schools will provide original typescripts of dissertations (or other research papers) on interlibrary loan. Therefore, if your library does not already own copies of the dissertations pertinent to your own topic, they may have to be purchased or possibly borrowed from the library of a school which is not the point of origin.

The dissertations which are available from Xerox University Microfilms are keyed to a voluminous publication with an imposing title: *Dissertation Abstracts International* (Ann Arbor, MI: Xerox University Microfilms, 1935– ). First called *Microfilm Abstracts* (vols. 1–11, 1935–51), later *Dissertation Abstracts* (vols. 12–29, 1952–69), *DAI* (the common initialism) publishes abstracts, or summaries (often rather lengthy), of doctoral dissertations written by the authors themselves and submitted by more than 350 cooperating institutions of higher learning; more than 30,000 titles are added annually. Monthly compilations are classified by broad subject areas and are published in two sections: A (humanities and social sciences) and B (natural sciences and engineering). Music, of course, appears in the former. Author and subject indexes are cumulated annually. Superseding these annual indexes for the period up to 1972, and indexing nearly all American dissertations for that period, is this extremely useful (but very expensive) thirty-seven volume tool: *Comprehensive Dissertation Index, 1861–1972* (Ann Arbor, MI: Xerox University Microfilms, 1973). Music, with an estimated 24,000 entries, is included in volume 31.

## A Practical Example

After all this discussion of dissertation indexes and abstracts, you are perhaps eager to learn how they may be put to use. Suppose you wanted to see if any dissertations on Debussy or Stravinsky were pertinent to your present topic. If your library has the *Comprehensive Dissertation Index*, you should have no trouble in looking up either composer in the subject index, which is organized according to key words in titles. If the titles you find have appeared in *DAI*, the volume and page numbers will be given.

If the *Comprehensive Dissertation Index* is not in your library, try the Adkins and Dickinson *International Index*, mentioned earlier. You will find here, in the index, no fewer than thirty titles listed under Debussy (p. 324) and thirty-two under Stravinsky (p. 368). There is no convenient overlap among these index entries indicating one or more works which deal with *both* Debussy and Stravinsky, but, even so, some further investigation is in order. Go to the main body of the work and consider one of the Debussy citations: Raymond Park, "The Later Style of Claude Debussy" (Ph.D. dissertation, University of Michigan, 1966). FIGURE 33 shows the entry in the subject index and the actual citation. Intriguing? Definitely, because we have already focussed on the late works of Debussy as a possible area of in-

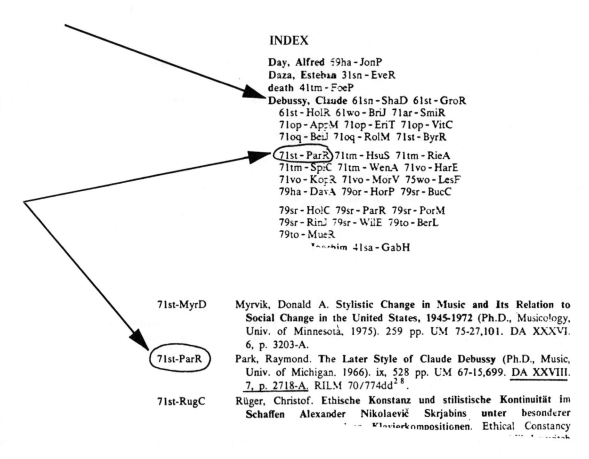

**INDEX**

Day, Alfred 59ha - JonP
Daza, Esteban 31sn - EveR
death 41tm - FoeP
Debussy, Claude 61sn - ShaD 61st - GroR
61st - HolR 61wo - BriJ 71ar - SmiR
71op - AprM 71op - EriT 71op - VitC
71oq - BeiJ 71oq - RolM 71st - ByrR
71st - ParR 71tm - HsuS 71tm - RieA
71tm - SpiC 71tm - WenA 71vo - HarE
71vo - KofR 71vo - MorV 75wo - LesF
79ha - DavA 79or - HorP 79sr - BucC

79sr - HolC 79sr - ParR 79sr - PorM
79sr - RinJ 79sr - WilE 79to - BerL
79to - MueR

Joachim 41sa - GabH

71st-MyrD    Myrvik, Donald A. **Stylistic Change in Music and Its Relation to Social Change in the United States, 1945-1972** (Ph.D., Musicology, Univ. of Minnesota, 1975). 259 pp. UM 75-27,101. DA XXXVI. 6, p. 3203-A.

71st-ParR    Park, Raymond. **The Later Style of Claude Debussy** (Ph.D., Music, Univ. of Michigan. 1966). ix, 528 pp. UM 67-15,699. DA XXVIII. 7, p. 2718-A. RILM 70/774dd[28].

71st-RugC    Rüger, Christof. **Ethische Konstanz und stilistische Kontinuität im Schaffen Alexander Nikolaevič Skrjabins** unter besonderer ... Klavierkompositionen. Ethical Constancy

Figure 33. Adkins, Cecil, and Dickinson, Alis, eds. International Index of Dissertations and Musicological Works in Progress. Philadelphia: American Musicological Society, International Musicological Society, 1977.

quiry. The abstract for this dissertation, readily found in *Dissertation Abstracts* (vol. 28, no. 7, p. 2718–A), describes stylistic traits in a limited number of Debussy's compositions from the period of about 1908–17. Among them is the work for two pianos mentioned earlier, *En blanc et noir*, which you will recall includes one movement (the third) dedicated to Stravinsky. The abstract and a subject entry from the same volume appear in FIGURE 34.

To explore this point further, you would, of course, need access to the dissertation itself. If your library does have it, be certain to check not only the text, but the bibliography also. Bibliographies in recent dissertations are frequently extensive and up-to-date. For research purposes, they may be as useful as the text itself.

### Foreign Dissertations

If you were looking for American dissertations only, in most cases you would have to go no further than *DAI*, which you would use along with the *Comprehensive Dissertation Index* and its supplements. But we have already established

the fact that foreign language materials are important for musical research, so logic compels us to consider a few of the more important sources which list foreign dissertations. The new Adkins and Dickinson *International Index* has already been mentioned. It includes 1,495 titles submitted by researchers and universities outside the United States and Canada.

A significant listing of 2,819 dissertations in the German language from universities in Germany, Austria, Switzerland, and Sweden is Richard Schaal, *Verzeichnis deutschsprachiger musikwissenschaftlicher Dissertationen 1861--1960 (Index of Musicological Dissertations in the German Language 1861--1960)* (Kassel: Bärenreiter, 1963). A supplement with 1,270 titles has been issued by the same author as *Verzeichnis deutschsprachiger musikwissenschaftlicher Dissertationen 1961--1970; mit Ergänzungen zum Verzeichnis 1861--1960 ( . . . ; With Material Supplementing the Index for 1861--1960)* (Kassel: Bärenreiter, 1974). The subject indexes of these volumes show that Debussy outranks Stravinsky as a dissertation topic (there are ten dissertations on Debussy, three on Stravinsky).

French dissertations are reported in a title recently pub-

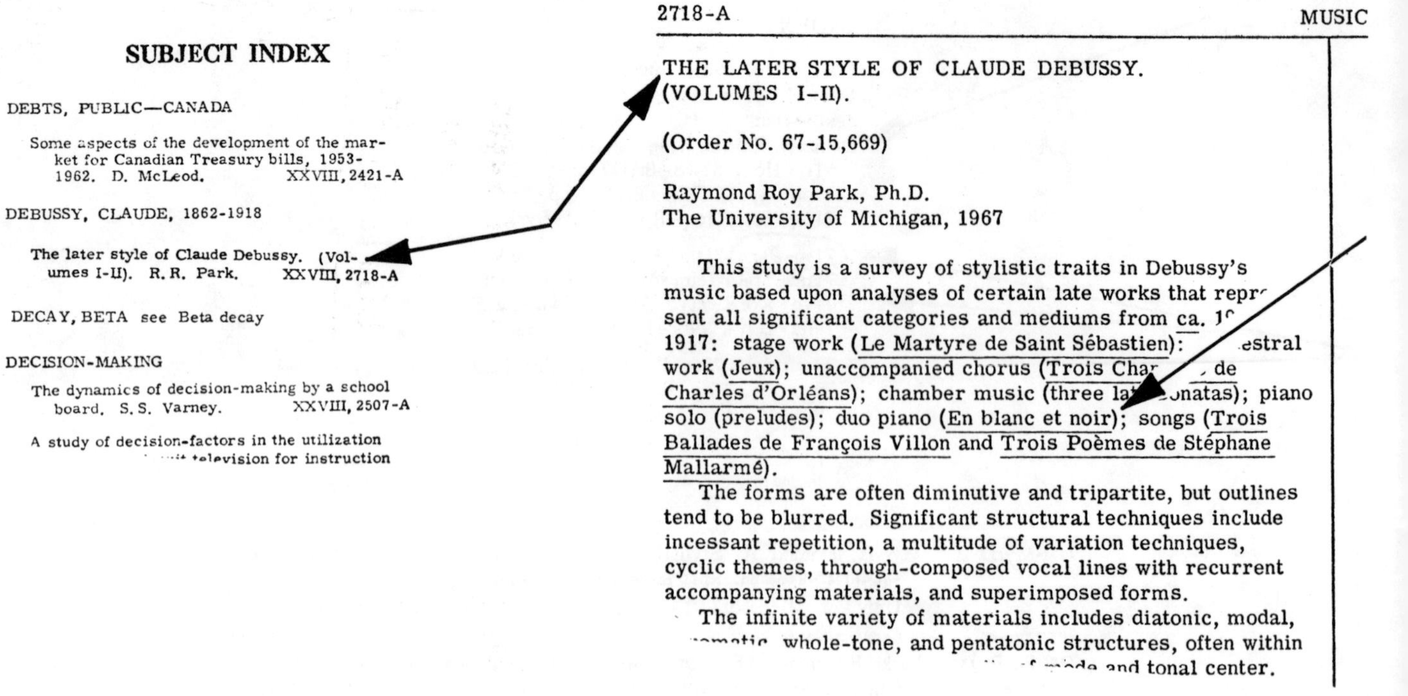

## SUBJECT INDEX

DEBTS, PUBLIC—CANADA

    Some aspects of the development of the mar-
       ket for Canadian Treasury bills, 1953-
       1962. D. McLeod.     XXVIII, 2421-A

DEBUSSY, CLAUDE, 1862-1918

    The later style of Claude Debussy. (Vol-
       umes I-II). R. R. Park.   XXVIII, 2718-A

DECAY, BETA see Beta decay

DECISION-MAKING

    The dynamics of decision-making by a school
       board. S. S. Varney.     XXVIII, 2507-A

    A study of decision-factors in the utilization
           television for instruction

THE LATER STYLE OF CLAUDE DEBUSSY.
(VOLUMES I-II).

(Order No. 67-15,669)

Raymond Roy Park, Ph.D.
The University of Michigan, 1967

    This study is a survey of stylistic traits in Debussy's music based upon analyses of certain late works that repr sent all significant categories and mediums from ca. 1917: stage work (Le Martyre de Saint Sébastien): estral work (Jeux); unaccompanied chorus (Trois Cha de Charles d'Orléans); chamber music (three l natas); piano solo (preludes); duo piano (En blanc et noir); songs (Trois Ballades de François Villon and Trois Poèmes de Stéphane Mallarmé).
    The forms are often diminutive and tripartite, but outlines tend to be blurred. Significant structural techniques include incessant repetition, a multitude of variation techniques, cyclic themes, through-composed vocal lines with recurrent accompanying materials, and superimposed forms.
    The infinite variety of materials includes diatonic, modal, matic whole-tone, and pentatonic structures, often within de and tonal center.

**Figure 34. Dissertation Abstracts.**

---

lished: Jean Gribenski, comp., *French Language Dissertations in Music: An Annotated Bibliography* (New York: Pendragon Press, 1979). Among the 438 titles listed here, there are seven which deal with Debussy and four with Stravinsky. The index identifies one which covers aspects of both composers: Ruth Moser, "L'impressionism français. Peinture, littérature, musique" ("French Impressionism: Painting, Literature, Music") (University of Geneva, 1952), described in citation 83.01 (pp. 177–178). FIGURE 35 shows the index entries and the citation. All annotations in this work are in French; titles are translated into English.

## Masters' Theses

    Sources of information on masters' theses are generally fewer and less available than those on doctoral dissertations, but they are still worth mentioning. Abstracts of selected theses from more than fifty American institutions are published quarterly in *Masters Abstracts: Abstracts of Selected Masters Theses on Microfilm* (Ann Arbor, MI: Xerox University Microfilms, 1962– ). As in the case of its companion

publication *DAI*, copies of the titles listed here are commercially available from the publisher.

    A project sponsored by the American Musicological Society resulted in the following list of 257 titles: Dominique-René de Lerma, *A Selective List of Masters' Theses in Musicology* (Bloomington, IN: Denia, 1970). The titles on Debussy (one) and Stravinsky (three) can be traced through the personal name index. The one most pertinent to your present topic is Sylvie Louise Koval, "Musorgsky and Debussy; A Study of the Creative Relationship" (M.M. thesis, Indiana University, 1964).

## Summary

1. Dissertations and theses are good sources of information, especially bibliographical information, and should not be overlooked.
2. Copies of most American dissertations and some masters' theses can be obtained commercially.
3. Reference tools listing foreign dissertations should be checked as a routine measure.

danse populaire
  Afrique, Haute-Volta, Mossi, *Liwaga*: 91.24
  France, Basse-Bretagne: 81.11
  —— Provence: 81.09
  rôle dans l'oeuvre de M. Ravel: 28.13
Debussy, Claude
  esthétique, relation avec l'impressionnisme:
    83.01
  —— nostalgie du XVIIIe s.: 27.28
  oeuvre, *Nuages*, analyse par ordinateur: 60.09
  —— *Préludes* pour piano, analyse sémiologique:
    60.13
  —— *Syrinx*, analyse sémiologique: 60.10
                      comparaison avec G. Fauré:
    82.16
  rôle de la musique dans son oeuvre: 62.00
  *Vie de Rossini*: 82.14
Stockhausen, Karlheinz
  oeuvre, *Momente*, analyse: 91.24
  style, musique vocale: 28.15
Strauss, Richard, vie, 1898-1918: 28.10
Stravinsky, Igor, esthétique: 83.01, 91.08,
  91.09, 91.10
string instrument building, *voir* lutherie
string quartet, *voir* quatuor à cordes
Suède
  chant populaire, thématique: 34.01
  compositeurs français, XVIe-XXe s.: 21.04
Suisse
  chant populaire, anthologie: 34.02
  Fribourg, proses en usage à l'église Saint-
    Nicolas, IXe-XVIIIe s.: 99.02
  —— vie musicale, 1750-1853: 26.09
  Genève, musique protestante, ca. 1540-55: 24.08
              musique et scolaire, XVIe-XVIIe s.:

# 83 Arts plastique

83.01
MOSER, Ruth
L'impressionisme français. Peinture, littérature, musique
[French impressionism. Painting, literature, music]
d, Lettres: Genève, 1952.
Genève, Droz, 1952: Lille, Giard, 1952; 285p. Mus., bibliog.,
index. [+Pn]

       Il est possible d'établir des correspondances entre les dif-
       férentes formes d'expression artistique, et par exemple
       d'opposer l'esthétique classique (peinture italienne de la
       Renaissance, littératures française du XVIIe siècle et al-
       lemande du XVIIIe siècle, musique allemande du XVIIIe siè-
       cle) à l'esthétique romantique du XIXe siècle. L'évolution
                                des arts. aboutit à l'im-
       ture, la musique au ...
       l'harmonie non plus de fonction tonale mais prise comme
       en soi en musique; l'anti-intellectualisme; l'esthétisme;
       l'absence de tout souci métaphysique; enfin l'amour de la
       nature, et surtout des sensations qu'elle inspire. L'esthé-
       tique impressionniste a provoqué, au début du XXe siècle,
       une réaction dont Stravinsky, en musique, est l'un des
       meilleurs illustrateurs.              *(Michel ROBERT-TISSOT)*

**Figure 35.  Gribenski, Jean, comp.  French Language Dissertations in Music.  New York:  Pendragon Press, 1979.**

"Simple was its noble architecture. Each ornament arrested, as it were, in its position, seemed to have been placed there of necessity."
– Voltaire (from *Le Temple du Goût*)

## The Imposing Dictum

In the course of your studies, you may have encountered, perhaps more than once, an imposing dictum concerning criticism and evaluation, such as "critical skills constitute a prerequisite to knowledgeable research." And you may have concluded that such pronouncements should be accompanied by trumpet fanfares and drum rolls, even though, you surmise, they have little application to your own work.

Let us dispatch the lofty rhetoric but retain the sentiment of the message. It is not an understatement to say that one of your most important and demanding tasks is to evaluate your source materials, especially those you depend upon most heavily. Some of this evaluation must be done on your own, and some can be done by consulting reviews and other reference materials which include scholarly appraisals.

As in the case of other skills, critical skills are advanced through use. In this chapter, we will be concerned with a few of the techniques through which you can begin to exercise these skills. By reading reviews, for example, you can learn what to look for, what experienced scholars have found important to comment upon. Judging a piece of writing on its external and internal features can also be learned. And finding out about an author's credentials can be helpful. Your goal will be to bring together various critical techniques in order to see how your source materials "stack up," so that you can use them most effectively.

## Reviews

Because outside evaluation (i.e., evaluation by someone other than the author) helps maintain scholarly standards, many if not most scholarly journals include book reviews as a regular feature. This is true in the field of music as it is in other disciplines. Some reviews of this kind are both descriptive and critical, often quite lengthy, and constitute significant essays in themselves. Other kinds of reviews — generally shorter and less erudite — serve mainly as aids for the selection of materials for libraries.

Reviews can be located in the same way as periodical articles, i.e., through the use of indexes. In fact, one of the major tools you used in compiling periodical references,

*The Music Index*, can also be used for finding book reviews; each monthly issue and annual cumulation carries a section under the subject heading "BOOK REVIEWS." The issue for August, 1976 (vol. 28, no. 8), for example, lists on pages 12–16 well over 200 book titles with review sources. Two books on Debussy are cited (but none on Stravinsky). FIGURE 36 shows these citations.

Two important general review indexes are *Book Review Digest* (New York: H.W. Wilson, 1905– ) and *Book Review Index* (Detroit: Gale Research, 1965– ). Both index *Choice* (Chicago: Association of College and Research Libraries, American Library Association, 1964– ) and *Library Journal* (New York: R.R. Bowker, 1876– ), which include reviews of books on music but are not themselves indexed in *The Music Index*. Although covering only about seventy-five review sources, *Book Review Digest* provides summarizing descriptions of the books under review and verbatim excerpts from many of the reviews cited. For example, the annual cumulation for 1975 includes (pp. 2–3) parts of two reviews of the Debussy bibliography by Abravanel, mentioned above. These reviews are shown in FIGURE 37. *Book Review Index*, which covers all reviews in over 250 periodical titles, indexes a few more titles in music than *Book Review Digest*.

Another major review index, *An Index to Book Reviews in the Humanities* (Williamston, MI: Phillip Thomson, 1960– ), provides coverage of about 270 periodical titles limited to the humanistic disciplines, including about ten in music (almost all of which overlap with *The Music Index*). The *Humanities Index*, mentioned in Chapter 4, may also be a good source, beginning with 1974. For newspaper reviews, probably the most useful tool is New York Times, *New York Times Book Review Index, 1896--1970*, 5 vols. (New York: Arno, 1973). For reviews after 1970, see *The New York Times Index*.

One of the best and most comprehensive sources of scholarly reviews in the field of music is *Notes: The Quarterly Journal of the Music Library Association* (Philadelphia: Music Library Association; first series, 1934–42; second series, 1943– ). Each issue includes lengthy reviews of significant books in music, plus a section devoted to reviews of music scores (including recent additions to historical series and composer editions in progress); another section provides an index to reviews of recordings. François Lesure's review of the Abravanel bibliography on Debussy (vol. 31, no. 2, pp. 290–291) is exemplary (irrespective of the inaccuracies

New acts. VARIETY 284:69 Aug 18 1976
DEAD BOYS, THE
    New acts. VARIETY 284:58 Aug 25 1976
DEAF SCHOOL, THE
    New albums: 2nd Honeymoon. MEL MAKER 51:18 Aug 21 1976
DEBUSSY, CLAUDE
    Claude Debussy. F. C. Ricci. See Ricci under BOOK REVIEWS
    Claude Debussy and the poets. A. B. Wenk. See Wenk under BOOK REVIEWS
    Works
        [Pelleas et Melisande] Glyndebourne. P. Griffiths and D. Fallows. MUS T 117:676-7 Aug 1976
        [Pelleas et Melisande] Glyndebourne Festival: Debussys "Pelleas" und Verdis "Falstaff." O. Trilling. il OPERNWELT
        n8:18-19 Aug 1976
        [Pelleas et Melisande] Hoehepunkte--"Eugen Onegin" und "Pelleas und Melisande" bei den Juni-Festwochen in Zuerich.
        I. Fabian. il OPERNWELT n8:12-13 Aug 1976
        [Preludes] Debussy and the Symbolist movement: the Preludes. A. P. Rafols. DIS ABST 37:683A Aug 1976
        [Quartet for strings, No. 1, Op. 10, G minor] A technical investigation and performance of three French violin sonatas
        of the early twentieth century (1915-1927), (Debussy, Ravel and Faure). S. Z. Rubinstein. DIS ABST 37:684A Aug
        1976
        [Sonata for violin and piano, No. 3, G minor] A technical investigation and performance of three French violin sonatas
        of the early twentieth century (1915-1927), (Debussy, Ravel and Faure). S. Z. Rubinstein. DIS ABST 37:684A Aug
        1976
DEBUT ORCHESTRA
    Young Musicians Foundation. HI FI/MUS AM 26:MA24 Aug 1976
DEES, RICK
    New on the charts ("Disco Duck (Part 1)"). biog port BB 88:26 Aug 21 1976
DEFLO, GILBERT
    Gala-Abende in Frankfurt. C. Natorp and C. Schwandt. ORPHEUS 3:695-6 n11 1975
DE GAETANI, JAN
    DeGaetani's Ives: up to all expectations (Nonesuch recordings). R. P. Morgan. port HI FI/MUS AM 26:84 Aug 1976
DEGEN, HELMUT
    Helmut Degen 65. biog port MH 27:67 n2 1976

                                    R. Nichols. MUS J 34:74 Jul 1976


Ranft, P. Felix Mendelssohn-Bartholdy--eine Lebens-Chronik. (Leipzig, Deutscher Verlag fuer Musik, 1973. 120p) R MUS
    ITAL 10:308-9 n2 1976
Ratz, E. Gesammelte Aufsaetze. Ed. by F. C. Heller. (Vienna, Universal, 1975. 168p DM 34,--) MELOS/NZ 2:242
    n3 1976
Rauhe, H. and others. Hoeren und Verstehen; Theorie und Praxis handlungsorientierten Musikunterrichts. (Munich, Koesel,
    1975. 247p DM 29,50) MUSICA 30:245-6 n3 1976
Regleski, T. A. Principles and problems of music education. (Englewood Cliffs, N.J., Prentice-Hall, 1975. 330p $10.95
    paper $6.95) CON MUS ED n4:107-13 Winter 1976
Repertoire International des Sources Musicales (International Inventory of Musical Sources), published by the International
    Musicological Society and the International Association of Music Libraries: A/I/5: Einzeldrucke vor 1800; Vol. 5,
    Kaa-Monsigny. Ed. by K. Schlager. (Kassel, Baerenreiter, 1975. 579p DM 200,--) AM RECORDER 17:39-40 n1 1976;
    R MUS ITAL 10:285-6 n2 1976
Ricci, F. C. Claude Debussy. (Bari, Adriatica, 1975. 340p) R MUS ITAL 10:286-7 n2 1976
Richter, C. Musik als Spiel--Orientierung des Musikunterrichts an einem fachuebergreifenden Begriff; Ein didaktisches Modell.
    (Wolfenbuettel, Moeseler, 1975. 271p DM 22,--) MUS U BILD 8:412 Jul-Aug 1976
Richter, K., ed. Istvan Kertesz. (Augsburg, Schroff-Druck. DM 29,80) MUSICA 30:249 n3 1976
Rothenberger, A. In mir klingt ein Lied. (Lichtenberg. 260p DM 22,--) ORPHEUS 2:722-3 n11 1974
Rudzinski, W. O muzyce przy glosniku. (Cracow, Polskie Wydawnictwo Muzyczne, 1975. 606p) RUCH MUZ 20:14-15
    n14 1976
Russo, W. Jazz composition and orchestration. (Chicago, Chicago Univ. Press. 825p paper $10.95) MUS ED J 62:81
    May 1976
Shacter, J. D. Piano man: the story of Ralph Sutton. (Chicago, Jaynar, 1975. 244p $7.95) ORK J 44:2 Jun 1976
Scheck, G. Die Floete und ihre Musik. (Mainz, B. Schott. DM 48,--) RECORDER & MUS 5:206 n6 1976
Schlepphorst, W. Der Orgelbau im westlichen Niedersachsen, Band 1: Orgeln und Orgelbau im ehemaligen Niederstift Muenster
    sowie in den Grafschaften Lingen und Bentheim. (Kassel, Baerenreiter, 1975. 339p) ARS ORGANI 24:2393 n50 1976
Schmeckel, C. D. The piano owner's guide. (N.Y., Scribner's, 1974. 127p $6.95) CLAVIER 15:6 n5 1976
Serle, G. From deserts the prophets come; the creative spirit in Australia 1788-1972. (Melbourne, Heinemann, 1973. 274p)
    MISC MUS 8:165-9 1975
Simosko, V. and Tepperman, B. Eric Dolphy: a musical biography and discography. (Washington, D.C., Smithsonian Institution
    Press. 132p $10.00) MUS ED J 62:69-70 May 1976
Simpkins, C. O. Coltrane: a biography. (N.Y., Herndon. 287p $7.95) JAZZ MAG (U S) 1:43 n1 1976; ORK J 44:30-31 Jun

                            (Atlantic Highlands, N.J., Humanities, 1976. 319p $15.00) MUS
    Schott. 60p
Wagner, K. Abbe Maximilian Stadler--Seine                                        160p $12.50) MUS
    Beitrag zum musikalischen Historismus im vormaerzlichen Wien.
    1976
Wangler, R. 6 Saiten 10 Finger; Grundlagen und Uebungen fuer Unterricht und Selbststudium des Klassischen, Spa...
    und begleitenden Gitarrenspiels. (Kassel, Baerenreiter) MENS EN MEL 31:253 Aug 1976
Watkins, G. Gesualdo: the man and his music. (London, Oxford Univ. Press, 1973. 334p P7.00) MELOS/NZ 2:244-5
    n3 1976; MISC MUS 8:161-4 1975
Weisberg, A. The art of wind playing. (Schirmer. P5.50) MUS T 117:657 Aug 1976
Wellesz, E. and Sternfeld, F., eds. The new Oxford history of music, Vol. 7: The Age of Enlightenment, 1745-1790. (London,
    Oxford Univ. Press, 1973. 742p P8.00) MISC MUS 8:148-52 1975
Wenk, A. B. Claude Debussy and the poets. (Berkeley, California Univ. Press, 1976. 355p $22.50) MUS J 34:58-9
    Jul 1976
Weston, P. The clarinet teacher's companion. (London, Hale. P2.00) MUS T 117:658 Aug 1976
White, J. D. The analysis of music. (Englewood Cliffs, N.J., Prentice-Hall, 1976. 190p $7.95) MUS J 34:59 Jul 1976
Wingenfeld, J. Und alle kamen nach Offenbach. (Offenbach, Bintz, 1974. 256p DM 38,--) ORCHESTER 24:435 Jun
    1976
Wolkenstein, O. von. Froelich geschray so well wir machen. Ed. by J. Heimrath and others. (Munich, Heimeran, 1975.
    124p DM 24,--) MH 27:114 n2 1976
Zanolini, B. Luigi Dallapiccola--la conquista di un linguaggio (1928-1941). (Padova, G. Zanibon, 1974. 95p) R MUS
    ITAL 10:287-8 n2 1976
BOOKER T. (r.n. Booker T. Jones)


**Figure 36. The Music Index.**

ABRAVANEL, CLAUDE. Claude Debussy: a bibliography. (Detroit studies in music bibl 29) 214p $9.50; pa $8 '74 Information Coordinators

016.78 Debussy, Claude—Bibliography
ISBN 911772-49-9 (pa)   LC 72-90430

The purpose of this bibliography is "to assemble books and articles in order to provide tools for research on Debussy and his music. . . . Reviews of only the most important books are included, generally only those appearing in musical or literary periodicals. Among the exceptions are reviews in daily newspapers of the first performances of the most important works. . . . [Bibliographical lists of the musical works themselves] are included in Chapter I. . . . I have [also] given details of the literary and personal activities of Debussy (Chapters VII and IX)." (Introd) Indexes.

"The compiler has not defined the limits of his research. But what matter? The main entries claim 169 pages (the remaining pages are given to exemplary indices). . . . And when the journals consulted include such hors de série items as Newsweek, Cuadernos Hispano-Americanos, Ongaku-Gaku, and Sovetskaia Muzyka, we have a concept of the depth of bibliographic research involved (as if the imprint were not a sufficient imprimatur). Abravanel has classified the listings most rationally so that this is a ready-access reference tool on a subject that fully merits such consideration. We need not belabor any potential shortcomings; this bibliography is worthy of any music collection and will prove invaluable to any scholar whose research even borders on the subject."
   Choice 11:577 Je '74 100w

"Here is the first systematic attempt to cover all of the literature devoted to Debussy. . . . This undertaking has been accomplished with exemplary care and will be of great usefulness. Debussy's musical works are not described, but his literary works are included. In other respects, no limitation appears a priori to have been kept to. . . . [Entries include] unpublished theses, dictionary and encyclopedia articles, [and] books containing a chapter or a substantial number of pages on Debussy. . . . The majority of entries, however, are evidently articles in journals. The 1,854 entries are divided into large bibliographic categories: general and biographical studies, studies of the works and their style, and Debussy's writing and correspondence. Several indexes . . . allow one to find items by authors' names. This plan has the merit of being clear, but it intermixes in each category two kinds of contributions: studies published during Debussy's lifetime . . . and those which appeared after his death." François Lesure
   Music Lib Assn Notes 31:290 D '74 850w

The ACADEMIC library: essays in ho— Guy R. Lyle; ed. by Evan I— Ruth Walling. 171p $6 '7' 027.7 Librar' Gu

Figure 37. Book Review Digest copyright (c) 1975, 1976 by The H.W. Wilson Company. Material reproduced by permission of the publisher.

in the citation pointed out below). Not only do you have a detailed assessment by a recognized authority on Debussy (credentials of authors will be discussed below), but you also are provided with a brief bibliography which supplements Abravanel and a notification about the establishment of the Centre de Documentation Claude Debussy in 1973. One item from this bibliography, pointed out in FIGURE 38, can be added to your stock of references on Debussy and Stravinsky: H. Hindlar [sic, should be Lindlar], "Debussymen [sic, should be Debussysmen] beim frühen Stravinsky," in Bericht . . . Kongress Basel 1962, pp. 252–253. (It must be

mentioned that the truncated title here is somewhat difficult to track down. The full title may be found in the National Union Catalog, 1956–67 cumulation, vol. 55, p. 258, under the heading "Internationaler Musikwissenschaftlicher Kongress. Kassel, 1962." It is as follows: Bericht über den Internationalen Musikwissenschaftlichen Kongress, Kassel, [not Basel] 1962. The NUC entry is shown in FIGURE 39. The point to be made here is that it sometimes takes a little digging to find the information you need. Seek help from your reference librarian if you run into a problem like this one!)

Other music periodicals with strong book review sections are the following:

Early Music (1973– )
Fontes Artis Musicae (1954– )
Journal of Music Theory (1957– )
Journal of Research in Music Education (1953– )
Journal of the American Musicological Society (1948– )
Melos: Zeitschrift für neue Musik (1920–34; 1946–)
Music and Letters (1920– )
Music and Musicians (1952– )
The Music Review (1940– )
The Musical Quarterly (1915– )
The Musical Times (1844– )
Die Musikforschung (1948– )
Revue de Musicologie (1942– )

Students whose libraries lack The Music Index may want to refer directly to these periodicals for reviews.

Reference books and other books which are encyclopedic in coverage, upon which so much research depends, are reviewed in American Reference Books Annual, edited by Bohdan S. Wynar (Littleton, CO: Libraries Unlimited, 1970– ). A section in each volume is devoted to music.

## The Outside and the Inside

After having consulted one or more reviews, you should try to assess a book in hand by determining if its external features show evidence of reliable scholarship. For example, does the text show ample documentation: are sources of information footnoted, mentioned in the text, or provided in a bibliography? Does it contain useful information in an appendix or glossary? Does the text contain musical examples or other illustrative material? Has it gone through two or more editions? (Landmark works are often updated and revised, thus indicating a wide acceptance by the scholarly community.)

On the subject of footnoting and the citation of sources, it must be said that the scholarly value of a piece of writing is not necessarily directly proportional to the number of citations, but a true sign of conscientious scholarship is the proper acknowledgment of sources and the provision of accurate bibliographical information concerning them. Actually, the practice of footnoting varies widely. The writings

**Claude Debussy: A Bibliography.** By Claude Abravanel. (Detroit Studies in Music Bibliography, 29.) Detroit: Information Coordinators, 1974. [214 p.; paper, $8.00]

Here is the first systematic attempt to cover all of the literature devoted to Debussy—a most necessary labor in view of the accumulation and world-wide dispersion of these writings, above all during the last twenty years and particularly on the occasion of the centenary in 1962. This undertaking has been accomplished with exemplary care and will be of great useful-

that of the musician's death, but also a date of significance to history.

One can observe a large disproportion between literature devoted to the man and his life, and that which concerns the works and their "language": the first prevails over the second, above all in the French works—and the classic monographs (Vallas, Dietschy, Lockspeiser) are not excluded from this remark. Perhaps the physiognomy of Debussy's *oeuvre* has changed too fifty years for anyone

would like, howe... important omissions (from prior to 1972, the date at which, it seems, this work was terminated): L. de la Laurencie, "L'orchestre de M. Debussy," *Le Guide musical* 49 (1903):810-11; Marion Bauer, "Impressionistic Methods: Debussy and His Influence," *Twentieth Century Music* (New York, 1933); Georges Lotes, "La poétique du symbolisme," *Revue des cours et conférences* (30 April 1934): 113 ff. [an analysis of Act IV, Scene 4 of *Pelléas*]; H. Hindlar, "Debussymen beim frühen Stravinsky," *Bericht . . . Kongress Basel 1962*, 252–53; E. Lockspeiser, "Debussy's Concept of the Dream," *Proceedings of the Royal Musical Association* 89 (1962/63):49-61; F. Lesure, "Retour à Khamma (Maud Allan-C. Debussy)," *Revue belge de musicologie* 20 (1966):124-29; E. Stilz, "Debussy und Ravel als wegbereiter ... Musik. Zyklische behandlung

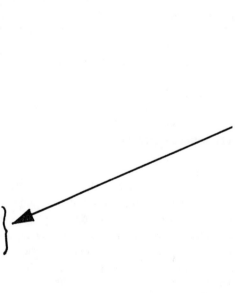

*lexikon* (Mainz, 1972), Kenneth Thompson, *A Dictionary of Twentieth-Century Composers 1911–1971* (New York, 1973), 77-116. One should not overlook certain annotations accompanying phonorecords, such as those by Pierre Boulez ("*Pelléas* Reflected") and Andre Schaeffner ("Debussy and the Theatre") which are included with the recording of *Pelléas* directed by Boulez (Columbia M3 30119).

Let us add, for those who are interested in the subject, that in 1973 the *Centre de documentation C. Debussy* was opened at 11 rue d'Alsace, Saint-Germain-en Laye.

FRANÇOIS LESURE
*Bibliothèque nationale, Paris*

Figure 38. Notes.

Kniznice hudebních rozhledů, 1963.
    430 p.  music.  25 cm.
    Contributions in Czech, German and Russian.
    1. Janáček, Leoš, 1854-1928.  2. Music-
Hist. & crit.—20th cent.  3. Music—Congresses.
NIC              NUC65-102679

**RL  I 0 50 542**

Internationaler Musikwissenschaftlicher Kongress.
    Kassel, 1962.
        Bericht über den Internationalen Musik-
wissenschaftlichen Kongress, Kassel, 1962.
Hrsg. von Georg Reichert [und] Martin Just.
Kassel, New York, Bärenreiter, 1963.
    xv, 392 p.  illus., port., facsims., music.
24 cm.
    At head of title: Gesellschaft für
Musikforschung.
    Bibliographical footnotes.
    1. Music—Congresses.    I. Reichert, Georg,
ed. II. Just, Martin, ed. II. Gesellshaft für
Musikforschung (Founded 1946)
NhD CSt NcU CtY-Mus      NUC67-90218

**RL  I 0 50 543**

Internationaler Nutzfahrzeug-Katalog.

**Figure 39. National Union Catalog.**

of some authors fairly bristle with citations, while others employ them rather sparingly. Of course, whether the text bristles or not can be due to the content: an original analysis of a musical composition may require few references, while a bibliographical study obviously demands extensive documentation.

You can also make a judgment by examining internal features, such as writing style and accuracy, but such a judgment often requires considerable experience if it is to be reliable. Perhaps you do have some literary acumen or a flair for detecting inaccuracies, in which case, by all means, proceed. It is not necessary (or possible, usually) to check all the facts, but you can be on the lookout for inconsistencies, instances of the *non sequitur*, and the like.

### The Author's Credentials

Checking on an author's credentials may be a simple matter for you if the author has published widely, less so, usually, if the author is not at all prolific, or is just getting started. (On the subject of determining an author's scholarly reputation, see also Chapter 3.) General biographical sources, such as *Who's Who in America* (Chicago: Marquis, 1899– ) and its British counterpart, *Who's Who* (London: Black, 1849– ) may be helpful. The *Directory of American Scholars*, 7th ed. in 4 vols. (New York: R.R. Bowker, 1978), which contains about 39,000 names, covers historians, including persons who have written on the history and theory of music, in the first of its volumes. In the international field, the *Dictionary of International Biography* (Cambridge,

England: Melrose, 1963– ) can be recommended; the tenth edition (1972) contains a complete index of names appearing in one or more editions from the first through the tenth. Also to be considered in this context are *International Who's Who* (London: Europa Publications, 1935– ) and *Who's Who in the World* (Chicago: Marquis, 1970– ).

Musical dictionaries and directories are also well worth consulting for biographical information. *The New Grove Dictionary of Music and Musicians* (1980), *Baker's Biographical Dictionary of Musicians* (6th ed.), the *Riemann Musik-Lexikon* (12th ed.), and *Die Musik in Geschichte und Gegenwart* list authors whose prominence is relatively recent as well as those who achieved recognition a generation or

more ago. Finally, there is a "Who's Who" for music that might possibly be useful: *The International Who's Who in Music and Musicians' Directory*, 9th ed. (Cambridge, England: International Who's Who in Music, 1980).

On the whole, evaluating materials indirectly on the evidence of the author's scholarly standing is less satisfactory than consulting reviews or making a judgment on your own, if you have a sufficient background. Indications of scholarly attainment (or lack thereof) may, however, corroborate one of the other approaches.

### Summary

1. Learning to develop your critical skills and evaluate your source materials is essential for effective research.
2. Reviews provide models for critical assessment as well as sources of critical information.
3. Through experience, you can learn to judge external and internal features of your materials.
4. An author's credentials may help complete a particular evaluation.

"Analysis is of little value if it is mere enumeration of statistics; such methods, frequently encountered in modern writings, overlook the synthetic element and the functional significance of the musical detail."
— Apel (from *Harvard Dictionary of Music*)

## History and Analysis

Music history and music theory are so closely connected that when one is developing a historical topic, such as the present one on Debussy and Stravinsky, it is not unusual that some theory will enter in. A common pattern for term papers and even advanced studies is to present a historical sketch along with an analysis of one or more compositions. Therefore it is important to know where to look for materials to support analytical work.

## Choosing a Method

You are probably well aware that there are many different approaches to analysis. Very few texts cover a broad spectrum of musical styles or present a comprehensive method pertinent to widely differing styles and various epochs. You can imagine that some aspects of analysis pertinent to the music of Palestrina would not be applicable to the works of Beethoven; and, likewise, one would not analyze Beethoven in exactly the same way as Debussy or Stravinsky. In addition, analytical texts vary from the elementary to the advanced, depending upon the audience for whom they were intended. You will want to choose one or more appropriate to your own background. It would be wise to check with your instructor about the methodology you intend to follow.

## Starting Points

If you have not had much experience in analyzing music, it would be beneficial for you to begin by reading the articles in the *Harvard Dictionary of Music* (2d ed.) on "Analysis" (pp. 36–37), "Style" (pp. 811–812), and "Style analysis" (p. 812). The last mentioned article was written by Jan LaRue, the author of *Guidelines for Style Analysis* (New York: W.W. Norton, 1970), one of the few textbooks which provide a comprehensive approach to the subject.

In the card catalog, you will find some useful subject headings, such as the following:
MUSIC—ANALYSIS, APPRECIATION

MUSIC—INTERPRETATION (PHRASING, DYNAMICS, ETC.)
MUSIC—ANALYTICAL GUIDES
Under the first of these you are likely to find a number of textbooks on music appreciation, as well as advanced analytical materials. The second heading points out analytical works written mainly from the point of view of the performer, and the third covers titles which present, for the most part, a series of analyses, usually of a limited repertory for a specific medium of performance (for example, piano music) or genre (for example, the symphony). In *The Music Index*, with which you became familiar in the earlier stages of your search, pertinent articles are listed under such headings as these:
ANALYSIS
CRITICISM
FORM
THEORY
FIGURE 40 shows how these headings appear on one page of *The Music Index, 1977 Subject Heading List* (Detroit: Information Coordinators, 1977), which is a separately issued guide to subject headings used in *The Music Index*.

## Specific Reference Tools

After you have surveyed the general field of analytical materials — it bears repetition that this phase of your research may be particularly important if you have not done much analysis — you can proceed to analyses of twentieth-century compositions. It is well known that for each of the broad epochs of Western music (beginning with the early Christian era and continuing through the medieval, renaissance, baroque, classical, romantic, and twentieth-century periods), a highly specialized vocabulary concerning specific aspects of musical style and composition has evolved. With regard to the music of this century, special dictionaries such as the following may help you over the terrain of unfamiliar terminology: John Vinton, ed., *Dictionary of Contemporary Music* (mentioned in Chapter 1); Robert Fink and Robert Ricci, *The Language of Twentieth Century Music: A Dictionary of Terms* (New York: Schirmer Books, 1975). Also, do not overlook the possibility that some twentieth-century

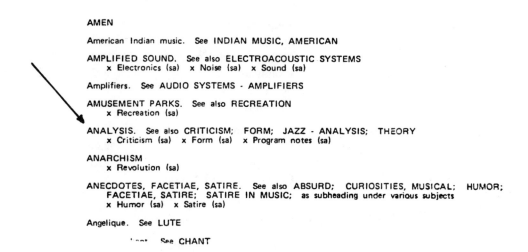

AMEN

American Indian music. See INDIAN MUSIC, AMERICAN

AMPLIFIED SOUND. See also ELECTROACOUSTIC SYSTEMS
  x Electronics (sa)   x Noise (sa)   x Sound (sa)

Amplifiers. See AUDIO SYSTEMS - AMPLIFIERS

AMUSEMENT PARKS. See also RECREATION
  x Recreation (sa)

ANALYSIS. See also CRITICISM;  FORM;  JAZZ - ANALYSIS;  THEORY
  x Criticism (sa)   x Form (sa)   x Program notes (sa)

ANARCHISM
  x Revolution (sa)

ANECDOTES, FACETIAE, SATIRE. See also ABSURD;  CURIOSITIES, MUSICAL;   HUMOR;
  FACETIAE, SATIRE;   SATIRE IN MUSIC;  as subheading under various subjects
  x Humor (sa)   x Satire (sa)

Angelique. See LUTE

‘---‘  See CHANT

**Figure 40. The Music Index.**

music texts may contain a special glossary, as in David H. Cope, *New Directions in Music*, 2d ed. (Dubuque, IA: Wm. C. Brown, 1976, pp. 237–243). FIGURE 41 provides an excerpt from this glossary and shows how it is listed in the table of contents.

Another of the reference tools on twentieth-century music that has particular relevance to the subject at hand is Arthur Wenk, comp., *Analyses of Twentieth-Century Music, 1940–1970* (Ann Arbor, MI: Music Library Association, 1975). The compiler here provides a convenient checklist of analytical articles and other materials (including books, *Festschriften*, and dissertations) published from 1940 to 1970 which concern the works of about 150 composers who died after 1900 (except for Bruckner, who is included, but who died in 1896); the articles appear in thirty-nine important music periodicals. Debussy and Stravinsky are well represented in this checklist, although no articles specifically linking the two composers are cited.

## Deciding on Compositions to Analyze

Unless your paper is to be mainly analytical, it is advisable to limit your detailed analyses to a small number of compositions. You may not have time to do otherwise. Just as it is impractical to try to read a large number of books in preparation for a term paper, it is nearly as impractical to attempt to cover a large number of compositions through analysis. In the case of Debussy and Stravinsky, limiting your detailed analytical remarks to one or two works by each composer would probably be acceptable.

The works you choose should be determined by the framework of the historical parts of your discussion and the points you wish to make concerning the relationship of the two composers. If, for example, you were to concentrate on

the Debussyan influences on the early works of Stravinsky, it would be appropriate to select Debussy's *Fêtes galantes*, second series (1904), set to poems by Paul Verlaine (1844–1896), and Stravinsky's *Poèmes de Verlaine*, op. 9 (1910). A comparison of these two sets of songs might give an indication of how deeply Stravinsky had absorbed, by 1910, some of the stylistic characteristics of impressionism. Or, you might wish to determine if there are musical aspects of Debussy's *En blanc et noir* (1915), third movement, which may have a bearing on the dedication, "à mon ami Igor Strawinsky" ("to my friend Igor Stravinsky"). Conversely, you could set out to determine what attributes of Debussy Stravinsky had in mind in writing *Zvezdoliki* (1912) and *Symphonies d'instruments à vent* (1920), both dedicated, as pointed out earlier, to the French composer.

If you have an extensive background in music theory and analytical methodology, it would be, quite possibly, a challenge to you to compare and contrast Debussy's *Jeux* and Stravinsky's *Le Sacre du printemps*, two ballets of the highest repute (and complexity) which were first performed in Paris in May of 1913 (*Jeux* on the fifteenth and *Le Sacre* on the twenty-ninth, both performances under the direction of Pierre Monteux); Debussy's work has remained somewhat overshadowed by *Le Sacre*, partially on the strength of the well-known riot which the latter provoked at its premiere.

## Finding a Model

Once you have selected the works to be analyzed and have examined the scores and listened to recordings of them, you will be ready for the writing of your analyses. For this phase of your work, it may be useful to use a model.

Among the most authoritative and conveniently organ-

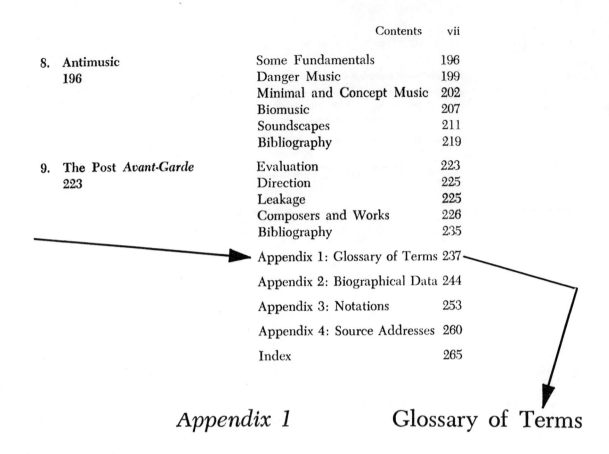

*Appendix 1*                Glossary of Terms

Here is an alphabetical listing of those terms used in the text which may need further clarification, with a brief definition of each. An asterisk (°) after a term within a definition signifies that the word so starred is itself defined within this glossary.

**amplifier:**  an instrument used to expand or increase the power of a sound or signal.

**amplitude:**  equivalent to the "loudness" of a pitch; the dynamics of sound.

**amplitude modulation (AM):**  a periodic variation of amplitude° creating tremolo.

**analog computer:**  a computer whose information is stored and processed using electromagnetic energy on wires or tapes, as opposed to a digital computer,° which employs numbers.

**antimusic:**  a term denoting those works the concept or implication of which is "opposed to" the traditional meaning of music. In current terms, it refers to those compositions which either (1) include no reference to sound in their scores; or (2) destroy one or more of the traditional composer/performer/audience relationships; or (3) are impossible to perform and exist only in concept.

... from tonality, or no tonality. Atonality is truly im-  ... by acoustical principles have  ... have

**Figure 41.  Cope, David H.  New Directions in Music.  2d ed.  Dubuque, Iowa:  Wm. C. Brown, 1976.**

ized analytical studies on individual compositions are the *Norton Critical Scores*. Each volume in this series — fourteen volumes have thus far appeared — contains a complete score along with a comprehensive analysis, plus supporting essays, commentaries, and other relevant materials. The volume on Debussy's *Prélude à l'après-midi d'un faune* (Prelude to the Afternoon of a Faun), edited by William W. Austin (New York: W.W. Norton, 1970), and Stravinsky's *Petrushka*, edited by Charles Hamm (New York: W.W. Norton, 1967), are of special interest with regard to your topic. Claudio Spies, a noted contemporary composer, has remarked in an article, "Editions of Stravinsky's Music," found in *Perspectives on Schoenberg and Stravinsky*, rev. ed., edited by Benjamin Boretz and Edward T. Cone (New York: W.W. Norton, 1972, p. 257), that the *Norton Critical Scores* edition of *Petrushka* is "the only existing corrected reprint" of the original (1912) version. (For early music, a series somewhat similar to the *Norton Critical Scores* was begun in 1977 by The University of North Carolina Press: *Early Musical Masterworks — Critical Editions and Commentaries*.)

## Musical Examples

The practical business of dealing with musical examples for your paper is covered rather thoroughly in Dwight D. Gatwood, *Techniques for Including Musical Examples in Theses and Dissertations: A Handbook* (Nashville, TN: Nashville Research Publications, 1970). Guidelines on this subject are also provided in Eugene Helm and Albert T. Luper, *Words and Music* (Hackensack, NJ: Joseph Boonin, 1971, pp. 24–27). Some schools have issued explicit requirements covering the format and identification of illustrative examples in term papers and other written assignments; be sure to find out if your music department or division has done so. Consistency is the watchword with regard to illustrations (and bibliographical citations as well).

## Postscript

It is well beyond the scope of this handbook to describe in detail various philosophies or methodologies of musical analysis. As you may have gathered from reading this chapter, it may be necessary for you to consult a number of materials before you find the method or model which seems most suitable for a particular term paper. Keep in mind that the same search techniques that you used in developing your topic are applicable in finding these materials.

## Summary

1. If you are writing on a historical topic, it is good to be prepared to do some analysis.
2. The procedures for finding analytical materials do not vary greatly from those for locating historical materials. General and special reference works, the card catalog, indexes, and bibliographies can all be brought into play.
3. For a term paper, the number of compositions to be analyzed is usually quite limited.
4. Analytical models should be considered.
5. Guidelines for including musical examples can be found in a few publications. In some instances, schools, divisions, or departments issue specific requirements for such illustrations.

"The eye is the painter and
the ear the singer."
— Emerson (from *Journals*,
1836).

## Enrichment

The field of music scholarship has been immeasurably enriched by developments in the fields of sound recordings and photography over the past hundred years or so. Through recordings, almost all students of music now have an opportunity to become acquainted with a range of art and traditional music, both Western and non-Western, which extends far beyond that normally provided in live performances. Furthermore, recordings afford a valuable opportunity for close comparison of different performances of the same work. And through facsimiles and microform reproductions, archival materials from around the world are made widely available. There can be no doubt that audio-visual resources have broadened the scope of music research.

## Recordings and Discographies

In pursuing your topic on Debussy and Stravinsky, it is likely that at some point you will need to devote some time to listening to those works you will be writing about. If your library has a substantial stock of cataloged recordings, you will probably find most of the works listed in the card catalog. However, you should be aware that cataloging practices for recordings vary somewhat from library to library, and you may not find individual entries for some works, particularly individual songs and brief instrumental or choral pieces. Your reference librarian will be able to show you how to track down such works through general headings and contents notes.

You may find it worthwhile to compile a list of recordings of those works discussed in your paper. The accepted term for such a list, or "bibliography of recordings," is discography. Several kinds of reference tools in addition to the card catalog will facilitate your search for pertinent recorded titles: (1) bibliographies of discographies, (2) catalogs of currently available recordings, (3) review publications, and (4) Library of Congress publications and computer data currently used for library cataloging purposes.

Akin to Besterman's *A World Bibliography of Bibliographies*, mentioned in Chapter 5, is this recent publication: David Edwin Cooper, *International Bibliography of Discographies: Classical Music and Jazz & Blues, 1962--1972; A Reference Book for Record Collectors, Dealers, and Libraries* (Littleton, CO: Libraries Unlimited, 1975). Like Besterman, Cooper provides a classified division of the subject matter, but Cooper does not follow his better-known counterpart by citing only separately published titles. For example, of the ten items indexed under Debussy, only one is a separately published discography, the others being periodical articles or monographs which include discographies. A similar series of citations can be found under Stravinsky, and special attention should be given to the comprehensive discography published by the Deutsches Rundfunkarchiv in 1972 (see citation no. C1043, shown in FIGURE 42). Another comprehensive bibliography has been published more recently: Michael Gray and Gerald Gibson, *Bibliography of Discographies*. Volume I: *Classical Music, 1925--1975* (New York: Bowker, 1977). Focusing on American, European, and Russian journal articles appearing between 1925 and 1975, it contains about 3,000 discographies. Debussy is found on pages 38–39 (citation numbers 831–856) and Stravinsky on pages 128–129 (citation numbers 2898-2939).

## "In-print" Guides for Recordings

If you have dealt very much with recordings, you have learned, no doubt, that many titles have a disconcertingly fleeting market life; some are reissued, often in various guises, but a considerable number are commercially available only for a few years or so, and then disappear from view, just as books become out of print. In order to keep up with this transitory situation, you must consult one or more current catalogs.

The family of catalogs known as "Schwann" is perhaps the most prominent group in the United States. The *Schwann-1 Record & Tape Guide* (Boston: W. Schwann, 1949– ), often called simply "Schwann-1" (former title: *Schwann Long Playing Record Catalog*) is a monthly publication which lists some 45,000 disc recordings, eight-track cartridge tapes, and cassettes. Serious music is arranged by composer. You should note that individual titles in some recorded anthologies are listed only at the first appearance in Schwann, in the "New Listings" section, as illustrated in FIGURE 43. In later appearances, a collective title is used, and the date of the first appearance serves as a cross-refer-

STRAVINSKY, IGOR, C63, C1042-
  C1051
Die Streichquartette der Wiener Schule;
  Schoenberg, Berg, Webern, C80
Streller, F., C907
Stricker, Rémy, C227
STRING BASSISTS, J271, J321-J322,
  J411, J498, J540-J542, J561-J562,
  J643
STRING QUARTETS [performing
  groups], C548
String quartets of Karol Szymanowski,
  C1058
Strong, Leonard Alfred George, C787
Struktur und Praxis neuer Musik im
  Unterricht; Experiment und Methode,
  C76

⋯⋯: C236

**Salome**

C1041  Mann, William. Opera on the gramophone: "Salome." *Opera*
       (England), VIII (July 1957), 420-25.

**STRAVINSKY, IGOR (Russian composer and conductor)**

C1042  Boonin, J. M. Stravinsky records Stravinsky; Stravinsky in print.
       *Musical America*, LXXXII (June 1962), 12-13.

C1043  Frankfurt am Main. Deutsches Rundfunkarchiv. Igor Strawinsky
       (1882-1971) Phonographie. Seine Eigeninterpretation auf Schall-
       platten und in den europäischen Rundfunkanstalten, zusammen mit
       einem Verzeichnis der in den deutschen Rundfunkanstalten
       vorhandenen Rundfunkproduktionen und historischen Schall-
       plattenaufnahmen von Strawinsky-Werken. Frankfurt am Main,
       Deutsches Rundfunkarchiv, 1972. 216 p. Preface in English, French
       and German.

C1044  Hamilton, David. Igor Stravinsky: a discography of the composer's
       performances. *Perspectives of New Music*, IX (=2, 1971), 163-79.

C1045  Hart, P. Stravinsky—just for the record. *Music Magazine*, CLXIV
       (June 1962), 42-47.

C1046  Odriozola, A. La discografia LP de Igor Strawinsky. *Musica* (Madrid),
       IV (#14, 1955), 139-54. In Spanish.

C1047  Philippot, Michel. Igor Stravinsky; l'homme et son oeuvre. Paris,
       Seghers, 1965. 188 p. In French. Discography: pp. 177-188.

C1048  Sopeña Ibáñez, Federico. Strawinsky: vida, obra y estilo. Madrid,
       ⋯⋯⋯ 1956, 270 p. In Spanish.

**Figure 42. Cooper, David Edwin. Internationl Bibliography of Discographies.**
**Littleton, CO: Libraries Unlimited, 1975.**

DEBUSSY—Continued
La Mer (1903-5) (Cont.)
   Szell, Cleveland Orch. † Ravel:Daphnis, Suite 2, Pavane
                                              Odys. Y-31928
Music of Debussy
   Ormandy, Smith, Bernstein, Entremont (6-70)
                          Col. MS-7523; ●16-11-0206
   Reiner, Munch, Gould, Pennario, Weissenberg (9-72)
                          RCA VICS-1668; ▲V8S-1044
Nocturnes (Nuages, Fêtes, Sirènes) (1893-9)
   Abbado, Boston Sym., NE Consv. Cho. † Ravel:Daphnis,
      Pavane                      DG 2530038; ●89419
   Ansermet, Suisse † Ravel:MaMère        Lon. 6023
   Barbirolli † Mer            Ang. S-36583; ●4XS-36583
   Boulez, New Phil. † Première; Printemps  Col. M-30483
   Boulez (see Orchestral)          3-Col. D3M-32988
   Dorati, Nat'l Sym., Cho. † Ibéria  Lon. 6968; ●5-6968
   Fournet, Netherlands Radio Phil.,Cho. † Ibéria Lon. 21104
   Giulini, Phil. Orch. † La Mer        Ang. S-35977
   Goberman, Vienna New Sym. & St. Op. Woman's Cho. †
      Jeux; Prélude              Odys. 32160226
   Martinon (see Orch.)    Ang. S-37067(Q); ●4XS-37067
   Munch, French Nat'l Radio Orch. † La Mer; Prélude
                          Turn. 34637; Vox ●CT-2119
   Temple U. Women's Cho. † Clair;
                              2-Col. MG-30950
                              Sera. S-60104
Petite Suite
   Ansermet, Suisse
   Eden & Tamir † Prélude, . .
      Trois morceaux
   W. & B. Klien † En; Fauré:Dolly
   A. & A. Kontarsky (see Piano)          2-DG 270...
   Martinon (see Orch.)          Ang. S-37064(Q); ●4XS-37064
Piano Music
   Ciccolini                      Sera. S-60253
   Cliburn (7-72)  RCA LSC-3283; ▲R8S-1268; ●RK-1268
   Entremont (4-61)                Col. MS-6214
   Frankl (complete)              6-Vox SVBX-5432/3
   Frankl (8) (5-67)                Turn. 34166
   A. & A. Kontarsky † Ravel:Piano    2-DG 2707072
   Moravec (3-69) † Pour: Ravel:Son.    Conn. S-2010
   Rubinstein (9-62) † Prokofiev:Visions; Szymanowski; Vil-
      la-Lobos:Prole        RCA LSC-2605; ▲R8S-5009
   Vasary (4-70)                  DG 139458
   Webster                    5-Desto 7111/5
Pour le piano (suite) (1896-1901)
   Beroff † Estampes; Images        Ang. S-36874
   Ciccolini (see Piano)            Sera. S-60253
   Entremont † Children's; Images    Col. MS-6567
   Moravec † Piano; Ravel:Sonatine    Conn. S-2010
   Vasary (see Piano)              DG 139458
Prélude à l'après-midi d'un faune (1892-4)
   Suisse † La Mer; Ravel:Rap. Lon. STS-15109
   Chabrier; Ibert; Ravel:Daphnis,
                          34500; ●MT-34500

NEW LISTINGS FOR JULY

Divertimento for Viola & Piano (1948)
   Thomas, Akst † Chihara; Stravinsky:Élégie
                                          Prot. 145
DEBUSSY, CLAUDE
   Clair de lune (from Suite bergamasque)
      Ormandy, Phila. Orch. (see Coll.)
                   RCA LSC-3284; ▲R8S-1269; ●RK-1269
   Piano Music
      Cliburn:Étude pour les octaves; Les terrasses
         des audiences au clair de lune; Clair de
         lune; La plus que lente; Jardins sous la
         pluie; Rêverie; Reflets dans l'eau; Feux
         d'artifice; La fille aux cheveux de lin; La
         soirée dans Grenade; L'Isle joyeuse
                   RCA LSC-3283; ▲R8S-1268; ●RK-1268
   Prélude à l'après-midi d'un faune
      Ormandy, Phila. Orch. (see Coll.)
                   RCA LSC-3284; ▲R8S-1269; ●RK-1269
   Preludes for Piano, Books 1 & 2
      Kars                      2-Lon. 2230
   Sonata No. 1 in d for Cello & Piano
      Frezin, Courtland † Franck:Son.; Ysaÿe
                                          Prot. 131

DES PREZ, JOSQUIN
   Sacred & Secular Works
      Burgess, Purcell Consort (F,I,L):Petite Ca-
         musette; Coeurs désolez; Déploration sur la
         ... de Johan Okeghem; ... Vive le roy; El
         ...  ... Fortuna

**Figure 43. Schwann--1 Record & Tape Guide.**

ence to the original listing.

The *Schwann-2 Record & Tape Guide* (Boston: W. Schwann, 1965– ; former title: *Schwann Supplementary Catalog*) is a semiannual listing covering monophonic, spoken word, and "non-current pop" recordings, in addition to other miscellaneous categories. Issued occasionally are the *Schwann Artist Issue*, the *Schwann Children's Record and Tape Guide*, and the *Schwann Country and Western Tape & Record Catalog*.

Complementing the Schwann catalogs is *The Harrison Tape Catalog* (New York: Weiss Publishing Corp., 1953– ), a bimonthly publication which lists as many as 20,000 pre-recorded tapes in various formats, including reel-to-reel, eight-track cartridge, cassette, and quadraphonic. The proportion of listings devoted to serious music is not nearly as large as in *Schwann-1*, and the contents of anthologies are not given.

Current European recordings are well covered in the following sources: *Gramophone Classical Catalogue* (Kenton, England: General Gramophone Publications, 1953– ), *Bielefelder Katalog* (Bielefeld, W. Germany: Bielefelder Verlagsanstalt KG, 1953– ), and *Diapason: catalogue général* (Boulogne, France: Diapason, 1964– ). Many of the recordings listed here are not readily available in the United States except through import dealers. The contents of anthologies are given in much more detail than in *Schwann-1*.

**Reviews of Recordings**

There are many publications devoted entirely or in part to reviews of recordings. Taking the lead among United States publications are the familiar periodicals *High Fidelity* (New York: Billboard Publications, 1951– ), which merged with *Musical America* in 1965; *Stereo Review* (New York: Ziff-Davis Publishing Co., 1958– ); and *American Record Guide* (New York: James Lyons, 1935– ). Among scholarly journals in the United States, *The Musical Quarterly* (New York: G. Schirmer, 1915– ) has carried reviews of recordings for many years. The longest-standing and probably most important review periodical is *The Gramophone* (Kenton, England: General Gramophone Publications, 1923– ); cross-references to reviews in this publication are found in the *Gramophone Classical Catalogue*, mentioned above. Other notable European periodicals carrying reviews are the following: *The Musical Times* (London: Novello, 1844– ), *Melos: Zeitschrift für neue Musik* (Mainz: Verlag B. Schott's Söhne, 1920–34; 1946– ), and *Musica: Zweimonatsschrift für alle Gebiete des Musiklebens* (Kassel-Wilhelmshöhe, W. Germany: Bärenreiter Verlag Karl Vötterle KG, 1947– ).

The most comprehensive index to record reviews is provided by *The Music Index*, a publication which has been mentioned a number of times in this guide. Antedating *The Music Index* by one year (1948) and providing somewhat more information, "discographically" speaking, is the featured column, "Index to Record Reviews," found in *Notes* (another publication which has been cited several times above). This column, edited by Kurtz Myers for many years, indicates by symbol the reviewer's opinion of each of the recordings cited. FIGURE 44 shows a listing of the recording shown earlier in its *Schwann-1* listing (FIGURE 43). The index citations are notably different from those in the *Readers' Guide*; for example, "● HF 10-72 p88" here means a neutral review found in the October, 1972, issue of *High Fidelity*, p. 88. A "+" indicates an excellent performance and a "–" indicates an inadequate performance. Recently published is a valuable multi-volume cumulation based on the "Index to Record Reviews:" Kurtz Myers, comp. and ed., *Index to Record Reviews* (Boston: G.K. Hall, 1978--80, 5 vols.).

CUI, CÉSAR: cf. Genesis GS-1004.

CUTTING, FRANCIS: cf. Musical Heritage Society MHS-1454.

DANDRIEU, JEAN FRANÇOIS: cf. Musical Heritage Society MHS-673.

DAQUIN, LOUIS-CLAUDE: cf. Musical Heritage Society MHS-673.

DAVIES, Sir HENRY WALFORD: cf. Odyssey 32-16-0318.

**DEBUSSY, CLAUDE ACHILLE**
Arabesques nos. 1 & 2; Estampes; Images—Books I & II. Hurnik, pf. Supraphon 111. 0699 (SD).
  +Gr 8-72 p355 (m.f.)
  +HF 3-72 p82
  +ML 7-72 p9

Estampes; Images—Books I & II; Pour le piano. Béroff, pf. Angel S-36874 (SD).
  +Gr 7-71 p204
  ●HF 1-73 p84
  +ML 5-71 p12
  +NR 12-72 p6
  +NYT 10-8-72 pD34
  +SR 12-2-72 p91
  ●St 4-73 p112

*My favorite Debussy:* Clair de lune. from Suite bergamasque; Étude pour les octaves; Feux d'artifice; La fille aux cheveux de lin; L'isle joyeuse; Jardins sous la pluie; La plus que lente; Reflets dans l'eau; Rêverie; Soirée dans Grenade; La terrasse des audiences au clair de lune. Cliburn. pf. RCA LSC-3283 (SD). (LC card—SD, 72-750005).
  ●HF 10-72 p88
  ●NR 10-72 p14

CF. ALSO: Angel S-36049 & S-36051; Deutsche Grammophon 2530.235; International Piano Library IPL505.

**DELIUS, FREDERICK**
Dance rhapsody no. 1; Eventyr—once upon a time; Paris—the song of a great city.

Figure 44. Notes.

## Other Sources of Information on Recordings

Information provided by the Library of Congress can be found in *Music, Books on Music, and Sound Recordings*, a title mentioned in Chapter 5. The 1973–77 quinquennial of this publication has recently been distributed. With regard to computer data on recordings, check with your reference or catalog librarian.

## Iconographies

The visual aspect of music — including everything from photographs of musicians to paintings and engravings of ensembles in performance to representations of instruments in the friezes of cathedrals or the illuminations of ancient manuscripts — is gaining interest as a subject of research and thus deserves a place in this guide. In 1971, under the joint sponsorship of the International Musicological Society (IMS), the International Association of Music Libraries (IAML), and the International Council of Museums (ICM), an organization known as *Répertoire international d'iconographie musicale* (RIdIM) was founded to deal with the field of musical iconography. Its headquarters, the Research Center for Musical Iconography (RCMI), was established at the Graduate Center of the City University of New York in 1972. RIdIM has inaugurated a series of iconographical publications (the first two numbers of which have appeared in microfiche), and RCMI currently issues the semiannual *RIdIM/RCMI Newsletter*, which carries information on a wide range of topics in the field.

You will have noticed in your search for materials on Debussy and Stravinsky that some books and articles are exceptionally well illustrated, for example, Minna Lederman, ed., *Stravinsky in the Theatre* (New York: Da Capo, 1975) or the article on Debussy in the *Encyclopédie de la musique*, published by Fasquelle (mentioned in Chapter 2). In fact, you may already have encountered the one photograph of Debussy and Stravinsky together that has been reproduced in various publications (more about this below).

At present, the most richly illustrated reference tool in music is *Die Musik in Geschichte und Gegenwart*, which has been noted previously. Also exceptional in this respect is the currently-in-progress *Sohlmans Musiklexikon*, 2d ed. (Stockholm: Sohlmans Förlag, 1975– ), a prominent Swedish encyclopedia. And in the one-volume category, the following title is densely packed with miscellaneous illustrations, some of them rather quaint: Percy A. Scholes, *The Oxford Companion to Music*, 10th ed., edited by John Owen Ward (London: Oxford University Press, 1970).

A useful introduction to the subject of illustrations is found on pages 119--120 of J.H. Davies, *Musicalia: Sources of Information in Music*, 2d ed., rev. and enl. (Oxford, England: Pergamon, 1969). A very good bibliography on the iconography of music can be found on pages 400–401 of the *Harvard Dictionary of Music*, 2d ed. (1969), mentioned earlier.

The "old standard" anthology of musical illustrations is Georg Kinsky, *Geschichte der Musik in Bildern* (Leipzig: Breitkopf & Härtel, 1930), which, in its English version, is known as *History of Music in Pictures* (1st ed., London: Dent, 1930). Another notable one-volume anthology — comprising photographs from the important Bettmann Archive in New York along with text related to Paul Henry Lang, *Music in Western Civilization* (New York: W.W. Norton, 1941) — is Paul Henry Lang and Otto Bettmann, *A Pictorial History of Music* (New York: W.W. Norton, 1960).

The most comprehensive anthology now available is Heinrich Besseler and Max Schneider, *Musikgeschichte in Bildern* (Leipzig: VEB Deutscher Verlag für Musik, 1961– ), which is still in progress. For present purposes, however, the most useful multi-volume anthology (also in progress) is François Lesure, ed., *Iconographie musicale* (Genève: Éditions Minkoff, 1973– ), since it includes a volume devoted entirely to Debussy: François Lesure, *Claude Debussy* (vol. 4 of the series, published in 1975). Among the 165 plates included here is a reproduction of the photograph of Debussy and Stravinsky mentioned above (see the plate shown in FIGURE 45).

What can be learned from this photographic evidence? Debussy seems much the larger of the two men, although the comparison is made difficult because Stravinsky is seated, while Debussy stands slightly in the background. And it is interesting to note that Stravinsky looks directly into the camera, in contrast to Debussy, who averts his gaze. Some intriguing, even if rather tenuous, psychological inferences could be drawn from this picture. According to Stravinsky, it was taken by Erik Satie (1866–1925), an eccentric French composer and friend of Debussy (see Igor Stravinsky and Robert Craft, *Expositions and Developments*; London: Faber and Faber, 1962, p. 138).

Containing even more plates (205) concerning Debussy than the Lesure publication is *Debussy: Documents Iconographiques*, introduction and notes by André Gauthier (Genève: Pierre Cailler, 1952). As for Stravinsky, an iconography covering the period up to 1920 is Theodore Stravinsky, *Catherine & Igor Stravinsky: A Family Album* (London: Boosey & Hawkes, 1973). Among these pages, you can find a picture of the composer at work on *Le Sacre du printemps* (Clarens, Switzerland, 1912). The most spectacular Stravinsky iconography — indeed one of the most important books on the composer to be published in recent years — was barely off the press at the time of this writing: Vera Stravinsky and Robert Craft, *Stravinsky in Pictures and Documents* (New York: Simon and Schuster, 1978). A special section on Stravinsky and Debussy is found on pages 61–66. The authors mention that Stravinsky once publicly acknowledged Debussy as "my father in music" (p. 63).

## Finding Illustrations

Finding specific illustrations with unusual subject con-

tent — a portrait of a lesser-known composer or a picture of a rare musical instrument — can be difficult, since there is no all-inclusive subject indexing available. One attempt at indexing the illustrations in a small number of journals over a short period of time can be found in Sara Yancey Belknap, *Guide to the Musical Arts: An Analytical Index of Articles and Illustrations, 1953--56* (New York: Scarecrow, 1957). The continuation of this title through 1968 is by the same author: *Guide to the Performing Arts, 1957--1968* (New York: Scarecrow, 1960–72).

A title mentioned previously, *RILM Abstracts of Music Literature*, provides subject indexing for books and articles having to do with iconography, but not for illustrations themselves.

In the card catalog, the subdivision — ICONOGRAPHY under names of persons will lead you to books comprising mainly plates and other illustrations, such as *Catherine and Igor Stravinsky*, mentioned above. Similar subdivisions under classes of persons (for example, MUSICIANS—PORTRAITS) or topical subjects (for example, MUSICAL INSTRUMENTS—PICTORIAL WORKS) may also be useful.

## Facsimiles

Published facsimiles, or photographic copies, of manuscript or printed music constitute an important segment of materials useful for study and research. Going back to the "original" — whether it be an example of early chant notation, a thirteenth-century codex containing motets, a set of printed part-books from the sixteenth century, an engraving of J.S. Bach's *Clavier-Übung, Part III*, or an autograph of a Beethoven piano sonata — can sometimes provide new insights into the creative process or shed new light on aspects of musical style and performance practice. Even for music of the twentieth century, facsimiles can play an important part in research. With regard to the present topic, you have the opportunity to compare a facsimile edition of a draft of Debussy's *Prélude à l'après midi d'un faune* (Washington, DC: The Robert Owen Lehman Foundation, 1963) with a printed version (for example, the edition by William W. Austin in the *Norton Critical Scores* series, mentioned in the previous chapter) to gain knowledge of the French master's technique of orchestration. A similar comparison can be made in the case of Stravinsky's *Le Sacre du printemps*: a facsimile of the sketches from 1911–1913 was published by Boosey & Hawkes in 1969; the full score was first published by both Édition Russe de Musique and Boosey & Hawkes in 1921.

## Microforms

Microforms (including microfilm, microfiche, and microcard reproductions) are by now a familiar part of the holdings of most academic libraries. Many newspapers, for example, may be available in the library only on 35-millimeter

Figure 45. Lesure, François. Claude Debussy. Genève: Éditions Minkoff, 1975.

microfilm, the most common of the microform formats. (Among newspapers of particular interest for musical coverage is *The New York Times*, which is indexed in *The New York Times Index, 1851--* , mentioned earlier.) Publications in microfiche (a type of microfilm in sheets, usually four inches by six inches) include composer editions, national monuments, and various multivolume texts of historical interest. Among significant microcard publications (microcards are opaque, usually three inches by five inches) is a series comprising theoretical treatises, issued by the Sibley Music Library of the Eastman School of Music at the University of Rochester (Rochester, New York).

For more advanced research, microform materials are often indispensable. Some libraries maintain an archive of these materials (usually microfilms) which have not been issued commercially. In some cases, special lists record the titles held (this information is not in all cases represented in the card catalog). Check with your reference librarian about the availability of such materials at your library or about obtaining them from other sources.

## Summary

1. Sound recordings and photographic reproductions have greatly enriched the field of music scholarship.
2. Discographies and "in-print" guides for recordings provide information about their availability, while reviews facilitate evaluation and comparison.
3. Visual aids, such as iconographies, facsimiles of musical manuscripts, and various microform publications, should all be considered potential sources of information.

> "Thus have you briefly those precepts which I think necessary and sufficient . . . ; but to have done it without being tedious unto you, that is to me a great doubt, seeing there is no precept nor rule omitted which may be any way profitable unto you in the practice."
> — Morley (from *A Plain & Easy Introduction to Practical Music*)

## The Answer

It is time to review your progress. But first, let us, for the sake of rounding out this narrative, pick up on a point left dangling near the outset. In Chapter 1, the question arose as to why Debussy disavowed any connection with the so-called "impressionist" school. It was this question that helped to stimulate the search in its beginning stages, and it is only fitting that some response to it be given now.

If you had actually worked on this topic, you would probably already have found a reasonable (if not "definitive") answer. For your background reading, you would most likely have consulted Oscar Thompson, *Debussy: Man and Artist* (New York: Dover Publications, 1967; unabridged and slightly corrected republication of the work originally published by Dodd, Mead, 1937). Thompson, as the first editor of *The International Cyclopedia of Music and Musicians* and the author of the article on Debussy in that reference work, appears to be a trustworthy source, and therefore you feel safe in attaching considerable weight to his discussion of Debussy and impressionism on pages 16–21. Thompson himself refers back to another biographer of Debussy, André Suarès, whose argument is summarized as follows (Thompson, p. 18):

> " . . . Debussy is a musical symbolist. One analogy is substituted for another. Instead of an art consanguinity to Monet and Renoir [impressionists], the brotherhood is with Mallarmé and Verlaine [symbolists]."

If Debussy's affinity to poetry and symbolism was greater than to art and impressionism, he was also a "solitary figure" (Thompson, p. 16), and his objection to being included in any kind of a "school," impressionist or not, is understandable from that point of view. Stefan Jarocinski, in *Debussy: Impressionism & Symbolism* (London: Eulenburg Books, 1976), feels that placing Debussy in the impressionist category has actually caused his music to be misunderstood (pp. 53–54):

> "The 'Impressionist' formula did not help but, on the contrary, hindered a proper appreciation of Debussy's music. It laid too much stress on the external and formal aspect of his works which, already, musicologists were unable to reveal in their true perspective so long as they continued to employ traditional methods."

We can speculate that Debussy anticipated misunderstanding of his music if it were labeled impressionistic, hence we have another possible reason for his objection to being called an impressionist.

## First Steps

The question about impressionism arose when you were looking for summarizing articles in music dictionaries and encyclopedias, the very important first step in your search strategy. As you continued your search, you became aware that refinement or narrowing down of the topic you had originally chosen was going to be necessary. The criteria for measuring the "breadth" and "depth" of a topic helped you to determine when your topic had reached an appropriate stage of refinement, and your background reading suggested some avenues to take.

## Good Fortune

You began your search at a point of interest and moved almost continuously toward a topic sufficiently limited to be covered in a term paper of moderate length. Good fortune accompanied you, for such smooth progress is not always possible. Occasionally, you will discover that some essential source materials for a particular topic are not available to you, or that the languages or analytical skills needed are beyond your ability. This may seem terribly unfortunate, but if the barriers are recognized at an early stage — and they *should* be if you are using a reasonably good search strategy — you can divert your search to a more fruitful area.

## Cards and Stacks

Only *after* you consulted some major dictionaries and encyclopedias, in order to see where your topic was leading, did you begin to collect references from the card catalog for your foray into the stacks of the general book and music score collection. While using the card catalog – the key to your library's book collection – you paid close attention to all of the information on the individual cards and learned to use that information to the fullest extent; you did the following: (1) checked for an indication of special bibliographies or appendices that might facilitate your search for further materials; (2) checked the subject headings at the end of the catalog entry to see if you were covering all areas of the card catalog where pertinent materials might be listed; (3) made a preliminary estimate of the value of each item that you looked up, and took special note of distinguished authors, important publishers, and up-to-date publications; (4) carefully recorded the *entire* call number so that you would be able to locate the item on the shelves. You also became familiar with the subject heading guide issued by the Library of Congress, since it is the source for the subject headings used in the card catalog (in most academic libraries).

Browsing through the general bookstacks where there were concentrations of materials pertinent to your topic, you were able to confirm your preliminary evaluations and were able to locate other materials of interest. Important parts of books were distinguished through chapter headings and listings of supplementary sections, such as appendices and bibliographies.

In the course of gathering all this bibliographical data, you began to compile a card file, in which you entered the data in accordance with the format suggested by your style manual. As you continued your search, you added notes and pertinent quotations to this file.

### Supplements

You recognized that there are very important – indispensable, in fact – supplements to the card catalog, supplements in the form of periodical indexes, bibliographies, and other tools, such as the computer. As you systematically investigated these resources, you enlarged your card file and at the same time began to formulate an outline for your paper in accordance with the content of the important books, articles, and essays that you were able to locate in your library. Those you were not able to locate were ordered on interlibrary loan as quickly as possible.

Thematic indexes, doctoral dissertations, and masters' theses were also investigated. You learned that some thematic indexes and other similar tools provide an overview of a composer's entire works; they supply a detailed framework, constructed mostly by chronology or genre, which facilitates the selection of works for analysis.

### Scrutinizing

In evaluating your source materials, you surveyed a number of important review indexes in order to locate re-

views, mostly in the periodical literature. You found that reviews can be important sources of bibliographical as well as critical and descriptive information. You also learned to examine, in a critical light, some of the source materials yourself, taking into account a few of the external and internal features that distinguish reliable scholarship.

In preparing to analyze a limited number of music scores for your term paper, you were able to see some of the problems inherent in this very important aspect of research: (1) analytical methods vary widely, and some are of considerable complexity; very few attempt to deal with the whole range of style in Western music; (2) special reference sources are required to define the vocabulary normally used to describe particular musical styles and compositional methods; (3) the analysis of some compositions, to be successful, requires rather well developed analytical skills gained from experience. (There are some reference tools which can help locate pertinent examples of analysis for you

66

to refer to and gather ideas from, but your own analyses should be the expression of your personal musical understanding, and in this sense should be, optimally, more creative than mechanical.)

### The Ear and the Eye

Finally, to conclude your survey of the reference sources for musical research, you examined some of the sources which list, index, or contain materials in the audio-visual area: sound recordings, reviews of recordings, pictures, facsimiles of music scores, and microforms. You had a brief introduction to the field of musical iconography. And you were persuaded, no doubt, that "the audio and the visual," far from being peripheral to research in music, are often essential.

### Contemplation

As you contemplate all of these research materials, their significance, and their application to your term paper, also keep in mind the human resources that are available to facilitate your progress. Your reference librarian, especially, will be able to show you how to use the resources in the library and how to obtain materials not in the library's collections. Your instructor, too, will be able to guide you in selecting and evaluating essential sources and in suggesting a methodology for analysis. Research should not be considered an activity in a vacuum; indeed, often it is a cooperative venture. If you have ever read the acknowledgment sections of some of the major research monographs in music (and in other disciplines also), you have observed that it is not exceptional for a number of persons to give aid in bringing a project to fruition. Of course, for your term paper, your consultation with others need not be widespread — if you keep in touch with your reference librarian and your instructor, your needs should be met.

### The Future

You have now arrived at the point where you are about to begin the writing of the paper or the drafting of detailed outlines, as you see fit. Your card file and the source materials you have selected should supply enough information to begin this task. What you have learned about reference tools and search strategy should be applicable to future term papers and perhaps to more advanced research. Although much attention has been paid to sources specifically related to music of the twentieth century, with emphasis on Debussy and Stravinsky, these sources are intended as illustrative examples having, in most cases, parallels or counterparts for other periods of Western music.

Finally, the objective of this guide is to assist you in selecting a topic appropriate to your own interests and abilities, through the use of basic reference sources, and to describe procedures whereby important source materials on this topic can be collected. To the degree that this objective has been met, you will be able to use this guide for future projects of a similar nature.

## LIBRARY USE QUIZ

PART A.

Directions: Refer to the catalog card in FIGURE A to answer the following questions.

```
ML        The unknown country
410
.S932     Tierney, Neil.
T55            The unknown country : a life of Igor
          Stravinsky / [by] Neil Tierney. London
          : Hale, 1977.
               272 p., [16] p. of plates : ill.,
          music, ports. ; 24 cm.
               Bibliography: p. [264]-265.
               Includes index.




               1. Stravinskiĭ, Igoŕ Fedorovich,
          1882-1971.  2. Composers--Biography.
          I. Title

OO                                        77-376232
```

**Figure A. Catalog Card.**

1. Would this card be filed with other cards beginning with the letters "TH," "TI," "ML," of "UN?"
2. What is the subtitle?
3. Is there a series title?
4. Does the book include a list of publications?
5. Under what other headings will cards for the book be found in the card catalog?

PART B.

Directions: Refer to the excerpt from the *Reader's Guide to Periodical Literature* in FIGURE B to answer the following questions.

6. How would you find the full title of the periodical which carries the article, "On Records; Pélleas et Mélisande?
7. What is the date of this article?
8. On what pages will it be found?
9. In what volume will it be found?
10. What is the subject heading for this article?
11. This excerpt lists reviews for what composition?

```
DEBUSSY, Claude
   Debussy on disc: 1912-1962. J. Holcman. il
     por Sat R 45:34-5 Ag 25 '62
   Debussy on microgroove; discography. por
     Hi Fi 12:66-9+ S; 84+ N '62

   Emancipator. il por Time 80:46 D 7 '62
   Heritage of Debussy; with editorial com-
     ment. F. Goldbeck. por Hi Fi 12:51, 52-5+
     S '62
   Imagery from without. A. Frankenstein. il
     por Hi Fi 12:59-62 S '62
   Inner unity; conversations with Ernest Anser-
     met on the art of Debussy. ed. by P.
     Heyworth. E. Ansermet. Hi Fi 12:56-8+ S
     '62
   Letter from Paris; hommages to the composer
     on centenary of his birth. Genêt. New
     Yorker 38:70-1 Jl 7 '62
   Marking the centuries: an anniversary and a
     survey of the future. M. Mayer. Esquire
     58:28 Ag '62
   Not likely to be equaled, let alone surpassed,
     by anyone; Ericourt's Debussy. R. Kam-
     merer. Am Rec G 28:633-4 Ap '62
   On records; Pelléas et Mélisande. J. W. Free-
     man. Opera N 27:36 D 29 '62
   Pelléas et Mélisande. Criticism
     New Yorker 38:203-4 D 8 '62
     New Yorker 38:64+ D 29 '62
     Opera N 27:24-5 D 29 '62
     Opera N il 27:14-16 D 29 '62
     Opera N il 27:17-19 D 29 '62
     Opera N il pors 27:8-13 D 29 '62
     Sat R 45:33 D 15 '62
   Quiet voluptuary. K. Hoover. il pors Opera
     N 27:8-13 D 29 '62
   Respectable Claude, the irreverent Achille.
     R. McMullen. pors Hi Fi 12:63-5+ S '62
   Still ecstatic about Debussy. H. C. Schonberg.
     il pors N Y Times Mag p20+ Ag 19 '62
DEBUTANTES
   Budding of young beauties. il Life 53:104-10+
     D 7 '62
   Cookie Cole meet-
```

**Figure B. Excerpt from the *Readers' Guide to Periodical Literature* (March, 1961 — Feb, 1963, p. 544).**

*Answers are given on the following page.*

# ANSWERS

## PART A.

1. "UN," for "unknown." This card would be filed according to the title. Initial articles ("a," "an," and "the," and equivalents in foreign languages) are ignored in filing.
2. A Life of Igor Stravinsky.
3. No series title is included.
4. Yes, on pages 264 to 265.
5. Under the author and two subjects:

   > Tierney, Neil
   > STRAVINSKIĬ, IGOR FEDOROVICH, 1882--1971
   > COMPOSERS — BIOGRAPHY

## PART B.

6. Look in the beginning pages of the *Readers' Guide,* where the abbreviations are listed. Most periodical indexes carry abbreviations at the beginning. In this case, the full title is *Opera News.*
7. December 29, 1962.
8. Page 36.
9. Volume 27.
10. DEBUSSY, Claude.
11. *Pelleas et Mélisande,* an opera. "Criticism" indicates reviews, usually of a particular performance.

If you got fewer than eight correct answers, you should study a guide such as Cook's *The New Library Key,* mentioned in the Preface, before proceeding with this book.

# BASIC REFERENCE SOURCES FOR COURSES IN MUSIC

Note: The first library search to be carried out with the following course-related reference sources will be made easier if they are used in conjunction with the main body of this book. An asterisk (*) designates a title cited in the text.

The cutoff date for most publications was 1979. Consult the card catalog as well as your reference librarian to see what works in this bibliography have been superseded by new titles or more recent editions.

## Outline

I.   Music History and Musicology
    A. The Discipline of Music History and Musicology
        1. Introductory Texts
        2. Selected Research Tools
        3. Dissertations and Theses
        4. Selected One-volume Histories
        5. Bibliographies
    B. Period Resources
        1. Antiquity
        2. Early Christian and Medieval Eras (to 1400)
        3. Renaissance Era (1400–1600)
        4. Baroque Era (1600–1750)
        5. Classical Era (1750–1800)
        6. Romantic Era (1800–1900)
        7. Twentieth Century
    C. Music in the Americas
    D. Iconography
    E. Ethnomusicology

II.  Music Theory; Analysis; History of Music Theory

III. Music Education

IV.  Performance; Performance Practice
    A. Solo Vocal Repertoire
    B. Solo and Small Ensemble Instrumental Repertoire
        1. Keyboard
        2. String
        3. Woodwind
        4. Brass
        5. Percussion
    C. Large Ensemble Repertoire
        1. Choral
        2. Instrumental
    D. Performance Practice

V.   General Reference Sources (useful for several courses)
    A. Music
        1. Encyclopedias; Dictionaries; Handbooks
        2. Bibliographies
            a. Music Literature
            b. Music
            c. Music Literature and Music
        3. Indexes
            a. Music Literature
            b. Music
        4. Directories
        5. Discographies and Other Audio-Visual Resources
        6. Research Guides
    B. General (not specifically musical)
        1. Bibliographies; Reference Guides
        2. Periodical Indexes
        3. Biography
        4. Reviews
        5. Library Research Guides; Style Manuals

## References

I.   Music History and Musicology

    A. The Discipline of Music History and Musicology

        1. Introductory Texts

Harrison, Frank Ll.; Hood, Mantle; and Palisca, Claude V. *Musicology*. Englewood Cliffs, NJ: Prentice-Hall, 1963. 337 pp.

Haydon, Glen. *Introduction to Musicology; A Survey of the Fields, Systematic & Historical, of Musical Knowledge & Research.*

Chapel Hill, NC: University of North Carolina Press, 1941. 329 pp.

Westrup, J.A. *An Introduction to Musical History*. London: Hutchinson House, 1955. 174 pp.

2. Selected Research Tools

Allen, Warren Dwight. *Philosophies of Music History: A Study of General Histories of Music, 1600--1900*. New York: Dover, 1962. 382 pp.

*Apel, Willi. *The Notation of Polyphonic Music, 900--1600*. 5th ed. Cambridge, MA: Medieval Academy of America, 1961. 464 pp.

*Brook, Barry S. *Thematic Catalogues in Music: An Annotated Bibliography*. Hillsdale, NY: Pendragon Press, 1972. 347 pp.

*Bryden, John R., and Hughes, David G. *An Index of Gregorian Chant*. Cambridge, MA: Harvard University Press, 1969. 2 vols.

Collaer, Paul, and Van der Linden, Albert. *Historical Atlas of Music*. Trans. by Allan Miller. Cleveland: World, 1968. 175 pp.

Coover, James. *Music Lexicography, Including a Study of Lacunae in Music Lexicography and a Bibliography of Music Dictionaries*. 3d ed., rev. and enl. Carlisle, PA: Carlisle Books, 1971. 175 pp.

Krummel, Donald William. *Guide for Dating Early Published Music: A Manual of Bibliographical Practices*. Hackensack, NJ: Joseph Boonin, 1974. 267 pp.

Spiess, Lincoln Bunce. *Historical Musicology: A Reference Manual for Research in Music*. Brooklyn: Institute of Mediaeval Music, 1963. 294 pp.

Strunk, Oliver. *Source Readings in Music History, From Classical Antiquity through the Romantic Era*. New York: W.W. Norton, 1950. 919 pp.

3. Dissertations and Theses

*Adkins, Cecil, ed. *Doctoral Dissertations in Musicology*. 5th ed. Philadelphia: American Musicological Society, 1971. 203 pp.

*Adkins, Cecil, and Dickinson, Alis, eds. *International Index of Dissertations and Musicological Works in Progress*. Philadelphia: American Musicological Society, International Musicological Society, 1977. 422 pp.

————————. *International Index of Dissertations and Musicological Works in Prog-*

*ress: American-Canadian Supplement (1979)*. Philadelphia: American Musicological Society, 1979. 62 pp.

*De Lerma, Dominique-René. *A Selective List of Masters' Theses in Musicology*. Bloomington, IN: Denia, 1970. 42 p.

*Gribensky, Jean, comp. *French Language Dissertations in Music: An Annotated Bibliography. (Thèses de doctorat en langue française relatives à la musique: bibliographie commentée.)* New York: Pendragon, 1979. 270 pp.

*Schaal, Richard. *Verzeichnis deutschsprachiger musikwissenschaftlicher Dissertationen, 1861--1960*. Kassel: Bärenreiter, 1963. 167 pp.

* ————————. *Verzeichnis deutschsprachiger musikwissenschaftlicher Dissertationen, 1961--1970*. Kassel: Bärenreiter, 1974. 91 pp.

4. Selected One-volume Histories

Borroff, Edith. *Music in Europe and the United States: A History*. Englewood Cliffs, NJ: Prentice-Hall, 1971. 752 pp.

*Grout, Donald Jay. *A History of Western Music*. 3d ed. New York: W.W. Norton, 1980. 849 pp.

*Lang, Paul Henry. *Music in Western Civilization*. New York: W.W. Norton, 1941. 1,107 pp.

Wörner, Karl H. *History of Music: A Book for Study and Reference*. 5th ed. Trans. and supplemented by Willis Wager. New York: Free Press, 1973. 712 pp.

5. Bibliographies

Brook, Barry S.; Downes, Edward O.D.; and Van Solkema, Sherman, eds. *Perspectives in Musicology*. New York: W.W. Norton, 1972. 365 pp. See: "Musicology as a Discipline: A Selected Bibliography," by Barry S. Brook, pp. 335--348.

Kahl, Willi, and Luther, Wilhelm-Martin. *Repertorium der Musikwissenschaft*. Kassel und Basel: Bärenreiter, 1953. 271 pp.

B. Period Resources

1. Antiquity

Mathiesen, Thomas J. *A Bibliography of Sources for the Study of Ancient Greek Music*. Hackensack, NJ: Joseph Boonin, 1974.

59 pp.

Sachs, Curt. *The Rise of Music in the Ancient World, East and West*. New York: W.W. Norton, 1943. 324 pp.

Wellesz, Egon, ed. *Ancient and Oriental Music*. London: Oxford University Press, 1957. 530 pp. Vol. 1: *The New Oxford History of Music*, edited by J.A. Westrup and others.

2.  Early Christian and Medieval Eras (to 1400)

Hughes, Dom Anselm, ed. *Early Medieval Music up to 1300*. London: Oxford University Press, 1954. 434 pp. Vol. 2: *The New Oxford History of Music*, edited by J.A. Westrup and others.

Hughes, Dom Anselm, and Abraham, Gerald, eds. *Ars Nova and the Renaissance 1300--1540*. London: Oxford University Press, 1960. 565 pp. Vol. 3: *The New Oxford History of Music*, edited by J.A. Westrup and others.

Reese, Gustave. *Music in the Middle Ages, With an Introduction on the Music of Ancient Times*. New York: W.W. Norton, 1940. 502 pp.

Seay, Albert. *Music in the Medieval World*. 2d ed. Englewood Cliffs, NJ: Prentice-Hall, 1975. 182 pp.

*Wolff, Arthur S. *Speculum: An Index of Musically Related Articles and Book Reviews*. Ann Arbor, MI: Music Library Association, 1970. 31 pp.

3.  Renaissance Era (1400–1600)

Abraham, Gerald, ed. *The Age of Humanism, 1540--1630*. London: Oxford University Press, 1968. 978 pp. Vol. 4: *The New Oxford History of Music*, edited by J.A. Westrup and others.

Brown, Howard Mayer. *Music in the Renaissance*. Englewood Cliffs, NJ: Prentice-Hall, 1976. 384 pp.

Krummel, Donald William. *Bibliotheca Bolduaniana: A Renaissance Music Bibliography*. Detroit: Information Coordinators, 1972. 191 pp.

Reese, Gustave. *Music in the Renaissance*. Rev. ed. New York: W.W. Norton, 1959. 1,022 pp.

4.  Baroque Era (1600–1750)

Bukofzer, Manfred F. *Music in the Baroque Era from Monteverdi to Bach*. New York: W.W. Norton, 1947. 489 pp.

Lewis, Anthony, and Fortune, Nigel, eds. *Opera and Church Music, 1630–1750*. London: Oxford University Press, 1975. 869 pp. Vol. 5: *The New Oxford History of Music*, edited by J.A. Westrup and others.

Palisca, Claude V. *Baroque Music*. Englewood Cliffs, NJ: Prentice-Hall, 1968. 230 pp.

5.  Classical Era (1750–1800)

Hill, George R. *A Preliminary Checklist of Research on the Classic Symphony and Concerto to the Time of Beethoven (Excluding Haydn and Mozart)*. Hackensack, NJ: Joseph Boonin, 1970. 58 pp.

Pauly, Reinhard G. *Music in the Classic Period*. Englewood Cliffs, NJ: Prentice-Hall, 1965. 214 pp.

Surian, Elvidio. *A Checklist of Writings on 18th-Century French and Italian Opera (Excluding Mozart)*. Hackensack, NJ: Joseph Boonin, 1970. 121 pp.

6.  Romantic Era (1800–1900)

Einstein, Alfred. *Music in the Romantic Era*. New York: W.W. Norton, 1947. 371 pp.

Longyear, Rey M. *Nineteenth-Century Romanticism in Music*. 2d ed. Englewood Cliffs, NJ: Prentice-Hall, 1973. 289 pp.

7.  Twentieth Century

Austin, William W. *Music in the 20th Century from Debussy through Stravinsky*. New York: W.W. Norton, 1966. 708 pp.

Cooper, Martin, ed. *The Modern Age, 1890--1960*. London: Oxford University Press, 1974. 764 pp. Vol. 10: *The New Oxford History of Music*, edited by J.A. Westrup and others.

*Cope, David H. *New Directions in Music*. 2d ed. Dubuque, IA: Wm. C. Brown, 1976. 271 pp.

*Deri, Otto. *Exploring Twentieth-Century Music*. New York: Holt, Rinehart and Winston, 1968. 546 pp.

*Fink, Robert, and Ricci, Robert. *The Language of Twentieth Century Music: A Dictionary of Terms*. New York: Schirmer Books, 1975. 125 pp.

*Karkoschka, Erhard. *Notation in New Music: A Critical Guide to Interpretation and*

*Realisation*. Trans. by Ruth Koenig. New York: Praeger, 1972. 183 pp.

*Salzman, Eric. *Twentieth-Century Music: An Introduction*. 2d ed. Englewood Cliffs, NJ: Prentice-Hall, 1974. 242 pp.

C. Music in the Americas

Anderson, E. Ruth. *Contemporary American Composers: A Biographical Dictionary*. Boston: G.K. Hall, 1976. 513 pp.

Chase, Gilbert. *A Guide to the Music of Latin America*. 2d ed., rev. and enl. Washington, DC: Pan American Union, 1962. 411 pp.

Historical Records Survey, District of Columbia. *Bio-bibliographical Index of Musicians in the United States of America since Colonial Times*. 2d ed. Washington, DC: Music Section, Pan American Union, 1956. 439 pp.

Hitchcock, H. Wiley. *Music in the United States: A Historical Introduction*. 2d ed. Englewood Cliffs, NJ: Prentice-Hall, 1974. 286 pp.

Horn, David. *The Literature of American Music in Books and Folk Music Collections: A Fully Annotated Bibliography*. Metuchen, NJ: Scarecrow, 1977. 556 pp.

Jackson, Richard. *United States Music: Sources of Bibliography and Collective Biography*. Brooklyn: Institute for Studies in American Music, Department of Music, Brooklyn College of the City University of New York, 1973. 80 pp.

Mead, Rita H. *Doctoral Dissertations in American Music: A Classified Bibliography*. Brooklyn: Institute for Studies in American Music, Department of Music, Brooklyn College of the City University of New York, 1974. 155 pp.

Napier, Ronald. *A Guide to Canada's Composers*. 1976 ed. Willowdale, Ont.: Avondale, 1976. 56 pp.

Orrego-Salas, Juan A. *Involvement with Music: Music in Latin America*. New York: Harper's College Press, 1976. 20 pp.

Sonneck, Oscar G.T. *A Bibliography of Early Secular American Music (18th Century)*. Rev. and enl. by W.T. Upton. Washington, DC: Library of Congress, Music Division, 1945. 617 pp.

Stevenson, Robert Murrell. *Renaissance and Baroque Musical Sources in the Americas*. Washington, DC: General Secretariat, Organization of American States, 1970. 346, 73 pp.

Weichlein, William J. *A Checklist of American Music Periodicals, 1850--1900*. Detroit: Information Coordinators, 1970. 103 pp.

Wolfe, Richard J. *Secular Music in America, 1801--1825: A Bibliography*. New York: New York Public Library, 1964. 3 vols.

D. Iconography

*Besseler, Heinrich, and Schneider, Max. *Musikgeschichte in Bildern*. Leipzig: VEB Deutscher Verlag für Musik, 1961– .

Brown, Howard Mayer, and Lascelle, Joan. *Musical Iconography: A Manual for Cataloging Musical Subjects in Western Art before 1800*. Cambridge, MA: Harvard University Press, 1972. 220 pp.

*Kinsky, Georg. *Geschichte der Musik in Bildern*. Leipzig: Breitkopf & Härtel, 1930. 364 pp. English version: *History of Music in Pictures*. London: Dent, 1930.

*Lang, Paul Henry, and Bettmann, Otto. *A Pictorial History of Music*. New York: W.W. Norton, 1960. 242 pp.

*Lesure François, ed. *Iconographie musicale*. Genève: Éditions Minkoff, 1973– .

E. Ethnomusicology

Gillis, Frank, and Merriam, Alan P., comps. *Ethnomusicology and Folk Music: An International Bibliography of Dissertations and Theses*. Middeltown, CT: Published for the Society for Ethnomusicology by the Wesleyan University Press, 1966. 148 pp.

Hood, Mantle. *The Ethnomusicologist*. New York: McGraw-Hill, 1971. 386 pp.

Kunst, Jaap. *Ethno-musicology: A Study of Its Nature, Its Problems, Methods, and Representative Personalities to Which Is Added a Bibliography*. 2d enl. ed. St. Clair Shores, MI: Scholarly Press, 1977. 158 pp.

Malm, William P. *Music Cultures of the Pacific, the Near East, and Asia*. 2d ed. Englewood Cliffs, NJ: Prentice-Hall, 1977. 236 pp.

Nettl, Bruno. *Folk and Traditional Music of the Western Continents*. 2d ed. Englewood Cliffs, NJ: Prentice-Hall, 1973. 258 pp.

————————————. *Reference Materials in Ethnomusicology*. 2d ed., rev. Detroit: Information Coordinators, 1967. 40 pp.

II. Music Theory; Analysis; History of Music Theory

Cooper, Paul. *Perspectives in Music Theory: An Historical-Analytical Approach*. New York: Dodd, Mead, 1975. 282 pp.

DeLone, Richard P. and others. *Aspects of Twentieth-Century Music*. Englewood Cliffs, NJ: Prentice-Hall, 1975. 483 pp.

Forte, Allen. *The Structure of Atonal Music*. New Haven, CT: Yale University Press, 1973. 224 pp.

*LaRue, Jan. *Guidelines for Style Analysis*. New York:

W.W. Norton, 1970. 244 pp.

Michelsen, William C. *Hugo Riemann's Theory of Harmony and History of Music Theory, Book III*. Lincoln, NE: University of Nebraska Press, 1977. 263 pp.

Riemann, Hugo. *History of Music Theory, Books I and II: Polyphonic Theory from the Ninth to the Sixteenth Century*. Trans. with commentary by Raymond H. Haggh. Lincoln, NE: University of Nebraska Press, 1962. 435 pp.

Slonimsky, Nicolas. *Thesaurus of Scales and Melodic Patterns*. New York: Coleman-Ross, 1947. 243 pp.

Ultan, Lloyd. *Music Theory: Problems and Practices in the Middle Ages and Renaissance*. Minneapolis, MN: University of Minnesota Press, 1977. 267 pp.

Wenk, Arthur, comp. *Analyses of Nineteenth-Century Music, 1940--1975*. Ann Arbor, MI: Music Library Association, 1976. 51 pp.

*————————, comp. *Analyses of Twentieth-Century Music, Supplement: 1940--1970*. Ann Arbor, MI: Music Library Association, 1975. 94 pp.

————————, comp. *Analyses of Twentieth-Century Music, 1940--1970*. Ann Arbor, MI: Music Library Association, 1975. 94 pp.

Williams, David Russell. *A Bibliography of the History of Music Theory*. 2d ed. Athens, OH: Accura Music, 1971. 58 pp.

III. Music Education

Collins, Thomas C., ed. *Music Education Materials: A Selected, Annotated Bibliography*. Washington, DC: Music Educators National Conference, 1968. 174 pp.

Ernst, Carl D., and Gary, Charles L. *Music in General Education*. Washington, DC: Music Educators National Conference, 1965. 223 pp.

Harris, Ernest E. *Music Education: A Guide to Information Sources*. Detroit: Gale Research, 1978. 566 pp.

Kaplan, Max. *Foundations and Frontiers of Music Education*. New York: Holt, Rinehart and Winston, 1966. 261 pp.

Leonhard, Charles, and House, Robert W. *Foundations and Principles of Music Education*. 2d ed. New York: McGraw-Hill, 1972. 432 pp.

Madsen, Clifford K., and Madsen, Charles H., Jr. *Experimental Research in Music*. Raleigh, NC: Contemporary, 1978. 116 pp.

Morgan, Hazel B., and Burmeister, Clifton A. *Music Research Handbook*. Evanston, IL: Instrumentalist, 1964. 110 pp.

Phelps, Roger P. *A Guide to Research in Music Education*. Dubuque, IA: Wm. C. Brown, 1969. 239 pp.

IV. Performance; Performance Practice

A. Solo Vocal Repertoire

Coffin, Berton. *Singer's Repertoire*. 2d ed. New York: Scarecrow, 1960–62. 5 vols.

Espina, Noni. *Repertoire for the Solo Voice*. Metuchen, NJ: Scarecrow, 1977. 2 vols.

Kagen, Sergius. *Music for the Voice: A Descriptive List of Concert and Teaching Material*. Rev. ed. Bloomington, IN: Indiana University Press, 1968. 780 pp.

*Nardone, Thomas R. *Classical Vocal Music in Print*. Philadelphia: Musicdata, 1976. 650 pp.

B. Solo and Small Ensemble Instrumental Repertoire

1. Keyboard

Arnold, Corliss Richard. *Organ Literature: A Comprehensive Survey*. Metuchen, NJ: Scarecrow, 1973. 656 pp.

Butler, Stanley. *Guide to the Best in Contemporary Piano Music: An Annotated List of Graded Solo Piano Music Published since 1950*. Metuchen, NJ: Scarecrow, 1973. 2 vols.

Hinson, Maurice. *Guide to the Pianist's Repertoire*. Edited by Irwin Freundlich. Bloomington, IN: Indiana University Press, 1973. 831 pp.

————————. *The Piano in Chamber Ensemble: An Annotated Guide*. Bloomington, IN: Indiana University Press, 1978. 570 pp.

*Nardone, Thomas R. *Organ Music in Print*. Philadelphia: Musicdata, 1975. 262 pp.

*Rezits, Joseph, and Deatsman, Gerald. *The Pianist's Resource Guide: Piano Music in Print and Literature on the Pianistic Art*. 2d ed. Park Ridge, IL: Pallma Music Co., 1978. 1,491 pp.

Spelman, Leslie P. *Organ Plus: A Catalogue of Ensemble Music for Organ and Instruments*. 2d ed. New York: American Guild of Organists, 1977. 37 pp.

2. String

*Farish, Margaret K. *String Music in Print*. 2d ed. New York: Bowker, 1973. 464 pp.

Grodner, Murray. *Comprehensive Catalog of Available Literature for the Double Bass*. 3d ed. Bloomington, IN: Lemur Musical Research, 1974. 163 pp.

Kenneson, Claude. *Bibliography of Cello Ensemble Music*. Detroit: Information Coordinators, 1974. 59 pp.

Loft, Abram. *Violin and Keyboard: The Duo Repertoire*. New York: Grossman, 1973.

2 vols.

Smet, Robin de. *Published Music for the Viola Da Gamba and Other Viols*. Detroit: Information Coordinators, 1971. 105 pp.

Vadding, M., and Merseburger, Max. *Das Violoncello und seine Literatur*. Leipzig: Verlag Friedrich Hofmeister, 1920. 172 pp.

Wilkins, Wayne, comp. *The Index of Viola Music*. Magnolia, AK: Music Register, 1976. 94 pp.

—————————, comp. *The Index of Violin Music*. Magnolia, AK: Music Register, 1973. 246 cols.

—————————, comp. *The Index of Violin Music (Winds), Including the Index of Baroque Trio Sonatas*. Magnolia, AK: Music Register, 1973. 38, 14 pp. Supplements, 1973– .

Williams, Michael D. *Music for Viola*. Detroit: Information Coordinators, 1979. 362 pp.

3. Woodwind

Alker, Hugo. *Blockflöten-Bibliographie*. 2d ed. Wilhelmshaven, W. Germany: Heinrichshofen's Verlag, 1966. 3 vols.

Houser, Roy. *Catalogue of Chamber Music for Woodwind Instruments*. 2d ed. Bloomington, IN: Indiana University Press, 1962. 159 pp.

Opperman, Kalmen. *Repertory of the Clarinet*. New York: Ricordi, 1960. 140 pp.

Pellerite, James J. *A Handbook of Literature for the Flute*. Rev. 3d ed. Bloomington, IN: Zalo, 1978. 408 pp.

Peters, Harry B. *The Literature of the Woodwind Quintet*. Metuchen, NJ: Scarecrow, 1971. 174 pp.

Rasmussen, Mary, and Mattran, Donald. *A Teacher's Guide to the Literature of Woodwind Instruments*. Durham, NH: Brass and Woodwind Quarterly, 1966. 226 pp.

Risdon, Howard. *Musical Literature for the Bassoon: A Compilation of Music for the Bassoon as an Instrument in Ensemble*. Seattle: Berdon, 1963. 24 pp.

Voxman, Himie, and Merriman, Lyle, comps. *Woodwind Ensemble Music Guide*. Evanston, IL: Instrumentalist, 1973. 280 pp.

Wilkins, Wayne, comp. *The Index of Bassoon Music, Including the Index of Baroque Trio Sonatas*. Magnolia, AK: Music Register, 1976. 76, 11 pp.

—————————, comp. *The Index of Clarinet Music*. Magnolia, AK: Music Register, 1975. 143 pp.

—————————, comp. *The Index of Flute Music, Including the Index of Baroque Trio Sonatas*. Magnolia, AK: Music Register, 1974. 131 pp. Supplements, 1974– .

—————————, comp. *The Index of Oboe Music, Including the Index of Baroque Trio Sonatas*. Magnolia, AK: Music Register, 1976. 96, 11 pp.

4. Brass

Beven, Clifford. *The Tuba Family*. London: Faber and Faber, 1978. 303 pp.

Brüchle, Bernhard. *Horn Bibliographie*. Wilhelmshaven, W. Germany: Heinrichshofen's Verlag, 1970. 272 pp.

Gregory, Robin. *The Horn: A Comprehensive Guide to the Modern Instrument and Its Music*. New York: Praeger, 1969. 410 pp.

—————————. *The Trombone: The Instrument and Its Music*. New York: Praeger, 1973. 328 pp.

Hohstadt, Thomas. *Solo Literature for the Trumpet*. Fullerton, CA: F.E. Olds & Son, 1959. 20 pp.

Morris, R. Winston. *Tuba Music Guide*. Evanston, IL: Instrumentalist, 1973. 60 pp.

Rasmussen, Mary H. *A Teacher's Guide to the Literature of Brass Instruments*. Durham, NH: Brass Quarterly, 1964. 84 pp.

Wilkins, Wayne, comp. *The Index of French Horn Music*. Magnolia, AK: Music Register, 1978. 120 pp.

5. Percussion

Combs, Michael F., comp. *Solo and Ensemble Literature for Percussion*. Terre Haute, IN: Percussive Arts Society, 1972. 66 pp.

Heller, George N. *Ensemble Music for Wind and Percussion Instruments: A Catalog*. Washington, DC: Music Educators National Conference, 1970. 142 pp.

C. Large Ensemble Repertoire

1. Choral

Burnsworth, Charles C. *Choral Music for Women's Voices: An Annotated Bibliography of Recommended Works*. Metuchen, NJ: Scarecrow, 1968. 180 pp.

May, James D. *Avant-garde Choral Music: An Annotated Selected Bibliography*. Metuchen, NJ: Scarecrow, 1977. 258 pp.

*Nardone, Thomas R.; Nye, James H.; and Resnick, Mark, eds. *Choral Music in Print*. Philadelphia: Musicdata, 1974. 2 vols. Vol. 1: *Sacred Choral Music*. 656 pp. Vol. 2: *Secular Choral Music*. 614 pp. *1976 Supplement*, edited by Thomas R. Nardone. 419 pp.

Tortolano, William. *Original Music for Men's Voices: A Selected Bibliography*. Metuchen, NJ: Scarecrow, 1973. 123 pp.

2. Instrumental

*Band Music Guide: Alphabetical Listing of Titles of All Band Music and Composers of Band Music*. 7th ed. Evanston, IL: Instrumentalist, 1978. 368 pp.

Carnovale, Norbert. *Twentieth-Century Music for Trumpet and Orchestra: An Annotated Bibliography*. Nashville, TN: The Brass Press, 1975. 55 pp.

Daniels, David. *Orchestral Music: A Source Book*. Metuchen, NJ: Scarecrow, 1972. 301 pp.

Eagon, Angelo. *Catalog of Published Concert Music by American Composers*. 2d ed. Metuchen, NJ: The Scarecrow Press, 1969. 348 pp. Supplement, 1971. 150 pp. 2d Supplement, 1974. 148 pp.

*Farish, Margaret K. *Orchestral Music in Print*. Philadelphia: Musicdata, 1979. 1,029 pp.

Kagarice, Vern. *Annotated Guide to Trombone Solos with Band & Orchestra*. Lebanon, IN: Studio P/R, 1974. 177 pp.

*Orchestra Music Guide*. Evanston, IL: Instrumentalist, 1966. 98 pp.

Saltonstall, Cecilia D., and Saltonstall, Henry. *A New Catalog of Music for Small Orchestra*. Clifton, NJ: European American Music Corp., 1978. 323 pp.

Satorius, Richard H. *Bibliography of Concertos for Organ and Orchestra*. Evanston, IL: Instrumentalist, 1961. 68 pp.

D. Performance Practice

*Donington, Robert. *The Interpretation of Early Music*. New version. London: Faber and Faber, 1974. 766 pp.

————————. *A Performer's Guide to Baroque Music*. New York: Scribner's, 1973. 320 pp.

MacClintock, Carol. *Readings in the History of Music in Performance*. Bloomington, IN: Indiana University Press, 1979. 432 pp.

Vinquist, Mary, and Zaslaw, Neal, eds. *Performance Practice: A Bibliography*. New York: W.W.

Norton, 1971. 114 pp.

V. General Reference Sources (useful for several courses)

A. Music

1. Encyclopedias; Dictionaries; Handbooks

a. General

*Apel, Willi. *Harvard Dictionary of Music*. 2d ed., rev. and enl. Cambridge, MA: Belknap Press of Harvard University Press, 1969. 935 pp.

*Baker's Biographical Dictionary of Musicians*. 6th ed., completely rev. by Nicolas Slonimsky. New York: Schirmer Books, 1978. 1,955 pp.

*Barlow, Harold, and Morgenstern, Sam. *A Dictionary of Musical Themes*. New York: Crown, 1948. 642 pp.

*————————. *A Dictionary of Opera and Song Themes, Including Cantatas, Oratorios, Lieder, and Art Songs*. New York: Crown, 1966. 547 pp.

Cobbett, Walter W., ed. *Cyclopedic Survey of Chamber Music*. 2d ed. London: Oxford University Press, 1963. 3 vols.

*Davies, J.H. *Musicalia: Sources of Information in Music*. 2d ed., rev. and enl. Oxford, England: Pergamon, 1969. 184 pp.

*Eitner, Robert. *Biographisch-bibliographisches Quellen-Lexikon der Musiker und Musikgelehrten der christlichen Zeitrechnung bis zur Mitte des 19. Jahrhunderts*. Leipzig: Breitkopf & Härtel, 1898–1904. 10 vols.

*Encyclopédie de la musique*. Publié sous la direction de François Michel en collaboration avec François Lesure et Vladimir Féderov. Paris: Fasquelle, 1958–61. 3 vols.

*Encyclopedie van de muziek*. Edited by L.M.G. Arntzenius and others. Amsterdam: Elsevier, 1956–57. 2 vols.

*Gatwood, Dwight D. *Techniques for Including Musical Examples in Theses and Dissertations: A Handbook*. Nashville, TN: Nashville Research Publications, 1970. 37 pp.

*International Who's Who in Music and Musicians' Directory*. 9th ed., edited by Adrian Gastner. Cambridge, England: International Who's Who in Music, 1980. 960 pp.

*Leuchtmann, Horst, and Schick, Philippine. *Langenscheidts Fachwörterbuch: Musik*. Berlin: Langenscheidt, 1964. 359 pp.

*Marco, Guy A. *Information on Music: A Handbook of Reference Sources in European*

*Languages*. Vol. 1: *Basic and Universal Sources*. Littleton, CO: Libraries Unlimited, 1975. 164 pp.

*Marco, Guy A.; Garfield, Ann M.; and Ferris, Sharon Paugh. *Information on Music: A Handbook of Reference Sources in European Languages*. Vol. 2: *The Americas*. Littleton, CO: Libraries Unlimited, 1977. 296 pp.

**Die Musik in Geschichte und Gegenwart. Allgemeine Enzyklopädie der Musik*. Edited by Friedrich Blume. Kassel und Basel: Bärenreiter, 1949–69. 14 vols. Supplements: vol. 15 (1973), vol. 16 (1979).

**The New Grove Dictionary of Music and Musicians*. Edited by Stanley Sadie. London: Macmillan, 1980. 20 vols.

*Pena, Joaquin. *Diccionario de la música Labor* Iniciado por Joaquin Pena, continuado por Higinio Anglés, con la colaboración de Miguel Querol. Barcelona: Labor, 1954. 2 vols.

Randel, Don Michael. *Harvard Concise Dictionary of Music*. Cambridge, MA: The Belknap Press of Harvard University Press, 1978. 577 pp.

**Riemann Musik Lexikon*. 12th ed., edited by Wilibald Gurlitt. Mainz: B. Schott's Söhne, 1959–74. 5 vols. Vol. 3 edited by Hans Eggebrecht; vols. 4 and 5 edited by Carl Dahlhaus.

*Scholes, Percy A. *The Oxford Companion to Music*. 10th ed., edited and rev. by John Owen Ward. London: Oxford University Press, 1970. 1,189 pp.

**Sohlmans Musiklexikon*. 2d ed. Stockholm: Sohlmans Förlag, 1975– .

*Thompson, Oscar, ed. *The International Cyclopedia of Music and Musicians*. 10th ed., edited by Bruce Bohle. New York: Dodd, Mead, 1975. 2,511 pp.

*Vinton, John, ed. *Dictionary of Contemporary Music*. New York: E.P. Dutton, 1974. 834 pp.

b.  Opera

*Kobbé's Complete Opera Book*. Ed. and rev. by The Earl of Harewood. New York: Putnam's, 1972. 1,262 pp.

Loewenberg, Alfred. *Annals of Opera, 1597–1940*. 3d ed., rev. and corrected. Totowa, NJ: Rowman and Littlefield, 1978. 1,756 columns.

Orrey, Leslie, and Chase, Gilbert, eds. *The Encyclopedia of Opera*. New York: Scribner's, 1976. 376 pp.

c.  Popular

Feather, Leonard. *The Encyclopedia of Jazz*. Rev. and enl. New York: Horizon, 1960. 527 pp.

Gentry, Linnell. *A History and Encyclopedia of Country, Western, and Gospel Music*. 2d ed., completely rev. Nashville, TN: Claimon, 1969. 598 pp.

Mattfeld, Julius. *Variety Music Cavalcade, 1620–1969: A Chronology of Vocal and Instrumental Music Popular in the United States*. 3d ed. Englewood Cliffs, NJ: Prentice-Hall, 1971. 766 pp.

Stambler, Irwin. *The Encyclopedia of Pop, Rock, and Soul*. New York: St. Martin's, 1974. 609 pp.

Stambler, Irwin, and Landon, Grelun. *Encyclopedia of Folk, Country, and Western Music*. New York: St. Martin's, 1969. 396 pp.

d.  Musical Instruments

Marcuse, Sibyl. *Musical Instruments: A Comprehensive Dictionary*. Corrected ed. New York: W.W. Norton, 1975. 608 pp.

*Musical Instruments of the World: An Illustrated Encyclopedia*. Edited by the Diagram Group. New York: Paddington and Two Continents, 1976. 320 pp.

2.  Bibliographies

a.  Music Literature

*Besterman, Theodore. *Music and Drama: A Bibliography of Bibliographies*. Totowa, NJ: Rowman and Littlefield, 1971. 365 pp.

*Bibliographia Musicologica: A Bibliography of Music Literature, 1968– *. Utrecht: Joachimsthal, 1970– . Annual.

**Bibliographie des Musikschrifttums*. Leipzig, Frankfurt am Main: Hofmeister, 1936– . Frequency varies; annual since 1960. Present publisher: B. Schott's Söhne, Mainz.

**A Bibliography of Periodical Literature in Musicology and Allied Fields and a Record of Graduate Theses Accepted*. Assembled for the Committee on Musicology of the American Council of Learned Societies by D.H. Daugherty. Washington, DC: American Council of Learned Societies, 1940. 135 pp. No. 1: October 1, 1938–September 30, 1939. Followed by: *A Bibliog-*

*raphy of Periodical Literature in Musicology and Allied Fields.* Assembled . . . by D.H. Daugherty, Leonard Ellinwood, and Richard S. Hill. Washington, DC: American Council of Learned Societies, 1943. 150 pp. No. 2: October 1, 1939--September 30, 1940. Ceased publication after two issues.

*Bobillier, Marie (Michel Brenet, pseud.). "Bibliographie des bibliographies musicales." In *L'Année musicale,* 3 (1913), 1–152. Reprint, New York: Da Capo, 1971.

*Duckles, Vincent. *Music Reference and Research Materials: An Annotated Bibliography.* 3d ed. New York: Free Press, 1974. 526 pp.

*Meggett, Joan M. *Musical Periodical Literature: An Annotated Bibliography of Indexes and Bibliographies.* Metuchen, NJ: Scarecrow, 1978. 116 pp.

*RILM Abstracts of Music Literature.* Edited by Barry S. Brook. New York: International RILM Center, 1967– . Quarterly.

Solow, Linda. *A Checklist of Music Bibliographies and Indexes in Progress and Unpublished.* 3d ed. Ann Arbor, MI: Music Library Association, 1974. 40 pp.

Swanson, Gerald L., ed. *Music Book Guide: 1974.* Boston: G.K. Hall, 1974. 120 pp.

b. Music

Brown, Howard Mayer. *Instrumental Music Printed before 1600: A Bibliography.* Cambridge, MA: Harvard University Press, 1965. 559 pp.

*Eitner, Robert. *Bibliographie der Musik-Sammelwerke des XVI. und XVII. Jahrhunderts.* Berlin: L. Liepmannssohn, 1877. 964 pp. Reprint, Hildesheim, W. Germany: Georg Olms, 1963.

Forsyth, Ella Marie. *Building a Chamber Music Collection: A Descriptive Guide to Published Scores.* Metuchen, NJ: Scarecrow, 1979. 191 pp.

Olmsted, Elizabeth H., ed. *Music Library Association Catalog of Cards for Printed Music, 1953--1972: A Supplement to the Library of Congress Catalogs.* Totowa, NJ: Rowman and Littlefield, 1974. 2 vols.

c. Music Literature and Music

*Bibliographic Guide to Music: 1975.* Boston: G.K. Hall, 1976. 470 pp.

*Bibliographic Guide to Music: 1976.* Boston: G.K. Hall, 1976. 477 pp.

*Bibliographic Guide to Music: 1977.* Boston: G.K. Hall, 1977. 477 pp.

*Bibliographic Guide to Music: 1978.* Boston: G.K. Hall, 1978. 506 pp.

Boston Public Library. *Dictionary Catalog of the Music Collection.* Boston: G.K. Hall, 1972. 20 vols.

British Catalogue of Music. London: Council of the British National Bibliography, British Museum, 1957– . Quarterly with annual cumulations.

*Charles, Sydney Robinson. *A Handbook of Music and Music Literature in Sets and Series.* New York: Free Press, 1972. 497 pp.

*International Inventory of Musical Sources. Series A, B, C.* [RISM.] München-Duisburg: G. Henle, 1960– .

*New York Public Library. Reference Dept. *Dictionary Catalog of the Music Collection.* Boston: G.K. Hall, 1964–65. 33 vols. *Supplement 1,* 1966. 811 pp.

*New York Public Library. Research Libraries. *Dictionary Catalog of the Music Collection: Cumulative Supplement, 1964--1971.* Boston: G.K. Hall, 1973. 10 vols.

*Notes: The Quarterly Journal of the Music Library Association.* Philadelphia: Music Library Association; first series, 1934--42; second series, 1943– . Quarterly.

*U.S. Library of Congress. *Music, Books on Music, and Sound Recordings.* Washington, DC: Library of Congress, 1973– . Semiannual with annual and quinquennial cumulations.

3. Indexes

a. Music Literature

*Belknap, Sara Yancey. *Guide to the Musical Arts: An Analytical Index of Articles and Illustrations, 1953--56.* New York: Scarecrow, 1957. Not paginated.

*——————. *Guide to the Performing Arts, 1957--* . New York: Scarecrow, 1960– . Annual.

Bull, Storm. *Index to Biographies of Contemporary Composers.* New York: Scarecrow, 1964. 405 pp.

——————. *Index to Biographies of Contemporary Composers, Volume II.* Metuchen, NJ: Scarecrow, 1974. 567 pp.

*Blom, Eric. *A General Index to Modern Musical Literature in the English Language, Including Periodicals for the Years 1915--1926.*

London: Curwen, n.d. 159 pp.

*Blom, Eric, and Westrup, Jack A. *Music and Letters: Index to Volumes I--XL*. London: Oxford University Press, 1962. 140 pp. Covers 1920–59.

Gerboth, Walter. *An Index to Musical Festschriften and Similar Publications*. New York: W.W. Norton, 1969. 188 pp.

*Goodkind, Herbert K. *Cumulative Index to the Musical Quarterly, 1915--59*. New York: Goodkind Indexes, 1960. 204 pp. *Supplement,1960--62*: New York, 1963.

*Krohn, Ernst C., comp. *The History of Music: An Index to the Literature Available in a Selected Group of Musicological Publications*. St. Louis: Baton Music Co., 1958. 463 pp.

*The Music Index: The Key to Current Music Periodical Literature*. Detroit: Information Coordinators, 1949– . Monthly with annual cumulations.

Tyrell, John and Wise, Rosemary. *A Guide to International Congress Reports in Musicology, 1900--1975*. New York: Garland, 1979. 353 pp.

b.   Music

*De Charms, Desiree, and Breed, Paul F. *Songs in Collections: An Index*. Detroit: Information Service, 1966. 588 pp.

Havlice, Patricia Pate. *Popular Song Index*. Metuchen, NJ: Scarecrow, 1975. 933 pp. *First Supplement*, 1978.

*Heyer, Anna Harriet. *Historical Sets, Collected Editions, and Monuments of Music: A Guide to Their Contents*. 2d ed. Chicago: American Library Association, 1969. 573 pp.

Hilton, Ruth B. *An Index to Early Music in Selected Anthologies*. Clifton, NJ: European American Music, 1978. 127 pp.

*Sears, Minnie Earl. *Song Index: An Index to More Than 12000 Songs in 177 Song Collections Comprising 262 Volumes*. New York: H.W. Wilson, 1926. 650 pp.

*————————. *Song Index Supplement: An Index to More Than 7000 Songs in 104 Song Collections Comprising 124 Volumes*. New York: H.W. Wilson, 1934. 367 pp.

Shapiro, Nat. *Popular Music: An Annotated Index of American Popular Songs*. New York: Adrian, 1964--73. 6 vols.

4.   Directories

Benton, Rita. *Directory of Music Research Libraries*. Preliminary ed. Iowa City: University of Iowa Press, 1967-- .

Musical America. *Annual Directory Issue*. Great Barrington, MA: ABC Leisure Magazines, 1968/69-- . Annual.

*The Musician's Guide: The Directory of the World of Music*. Chicago: Marquis Academic Media, 1980. 943 pp.

5.   Discographies and Other Audio-Visual Resources

*American Record Guide*. New York: James Lyons, 1935– . Monthly.

*Bielefelder Katalog*. Bielefeld, W. Germany: Bielefelder Verlagsanstalt KG, 1953– . Semiannual.

*Cooper, David Edwin. *International Bibliography of Discographies: Classical Music and Jazz & Blues, 1962--1972; A Reference Book for Record Collectors, Dealers, and Libraries*. Littleton, CO: Libraries Unlimited, 1975. 272 pp.

*Diapason: catalogue général de musique classique et de diction*. Boulogne, France: Diapason, 1964– . Annual.

*The Gramophone*. Kenton, England: General Gramophone Publications, 1923– . Monthly.

*The Gramophone: Classical Record Catalogue*. Kenton, England: General Gramophone Publications, 1953– . Quarterly.

*Gray, Michael H., and Gibson, Gerald D. *Bibliography of Discographies*. Vol. 1: *Classical Music, 1925--1975*. New York: R.R. Bowker, 1977. 164 pp.

*The Harrison Tape Catalog*. New York: Weiss, 1953– . Bimonthly.

*High Fidelity*. New York: Billboard, 1951– . Monthly.

*Myers, Kurtz, comp. and ed. *Index to Record Reviews*. Boston, G.K. Hall, 1978--80. 5 vols.

*Schwann-1 Record & Tape Guide*. Boston: Schwann, 1949– . Monthly.

*Schwann-2 Record & Tape Guide*. Boston: Schwann, 1965-- . Semiannual.

Sibley Music Library. *Catalog of Sound Recordings*. Boston: G.K. Hall, 1977. 14 vols.

Sibley Music Library. *Microform Publications, Fall 1976*. Rochester, NY: Sibley Music Library, Eastman School of Music, University of Rochester, 1976. 36 pp.

*Stereo Review*. New York: Ziff-Davis, 1958– . Monthly.

6. Research Guides

De Lerma, Dominique-René. *Involvement with Music: Resources for Music Research*. New York: Harper's College Press, 1976. 17 pp.

Garrett, Allen M. *An Introduction to Research in Music*. Washington, DC: Catholic University of America Press, 1958. 169 pp.

*Helm, Ernest Eugene, and Luper, Albert T. *Words and Music: Form and Procedure in Theses, Dissertations, Research Papers, Book Reports, Programs, and Theses in Composition*. Hackensack, NJ: Joseph Boonin, 1971. 78 pp.

Irvine, Demar B. *Methods of Research in Music. Part 1: Methods*. Seattle, WA (Ann Arbor, MI: Lithographed by Edwards Brothers), 1945. 69 pp.

*——————. *Writing about Music: A Style Book for Reports and Theses*. 2d ed., rev. and enl. Seattle: University of Washington Press, 1968. 211 pp.

*Mixter, Keith E. *General Bibliography for Music Research*. 2d ed. Detroit: Information Coordinators, 1975. 135 pp.

*Watanabe, Ruth T. *Introduction to Music Research*. Englewood Cliffs, NJ: Prentice-Hall, 1967. 237 pp.

Whalon, Marion K. *Performing Arts Research: A Guide to Information Sources*. Detroit: Gale Research, 1976. 280 pp.

B. General (not specifically musical)

1. Bibliographies; Reference Guides

*American Book Publishing Record*. New York: Bowker, 1960– . Monthly with annual cumulations.

Bell, Marion V., and Swidan, Eleanor A. *Reference Books: A Brief Guide*. 8th ed. Baltimore: Enoch Pratt Free Library, 1978. 179 pp.

*Besterman, Theodore. *A World Bibliography of Bibliographies*. 4th ed. Lausanne: Societas Bibliographica, 1965–66. 5 vols.

*Bibliographic Index: A Cumulative Bibliography of Bibliographies*. New York: H.W. Wilson, 1938– . Semiannual with annual cumulations.

*Books in Print*. New York: Bowker, 1948– . Annual.

*Comprehensive Dissertation Index, 1861–1972*. Ann Arbor, MI: Xerox University Microfilms, 1973. 37 vols.

*Dissertation Abstracts International*. Ann Arbor, MI: Xerox University Microfilms, 1935– . Monthly with annual cumulations. Former titles: *Microfilm Abstracts*, vols. 1–11 (1935–51); *Dissertation Abstracts*, vols. 12–29 (1952–69).

*Masters Abstracts: Abstracts of Selected Masters Theses on Microfilm*. Ann Arbor, MI: Xerox University Microfilms, 1962– . Quarterly.

*National Union Catalog*. Washington, DC: Library of Congress, 1956– . Printed in 9 monthly issues, 3 quarterly cumulations, annual cumulations for four years, and a quinquennial in the fifth.

*The National Union Catalog: Pre-1956 Imprints*. London: Mansell, 1968– .

Sheehy, Eugene P., comp. *Guide to Reference Books*. 9th ed. Chicago: American Library Association, 1976. 1,015 pp. Supplement, 1980. 305 pp.

*Subject Guide to Books in Print*. New York: Bowker, 1957– . Annual.

*U.S. Library of Congress. *Library of Congress Catalog – Books: Subjects; A Cumulative List of Works Represented by Library of Congress Printed Cards, 1950– *. Washington, DC: Library of Congress, 1955– . Three quarterly issues with annual and quinquennial cumulations.

*U.S. Library of Congress. *Library of Congress Subject Headings*. 9th ed. Washington, DC: Library of Congress, 1980. 2 vols.

Walford, Albert J., ed. *Guide to Reference Material*. 3d ed. London: Library Association, 1973–77. 3 vols.

2. Periodical Indexes

*British Humanities Index, 1962– *. London: Library Association, 1963– . Quarterly with annual cumulations.

*Humanities Index*. New York: H.W. Wilson, 1974– . Quarterly with annual cumulations. Preceded by the *Social Sciences & Humanities Index* (1965–74) and the *International Index* (1907–1965).

*International Index to Periodicals, 1907–65*. New York: H.W. Wilson, 1916–65.

*New York Times Index, 1851– *. New York: New York Times, 1913– . Semimonthly with quarterly and annual cumulations.

*Readers' Guide to Periodical Literature, 1900– *. New York: H.W. Wilson, 1905– . Semimonthly with quarterly and annual cumulations.

*Social Sciences & Humanities Index*. New

York: H.W. Wilson, 1965–74.

3. Biography

*Dictionary of International Biography*. 14th ed. Cambridge, England: Melrose, 1978. 2 vols.

*Directory of American Scholars*. 7th ed. New York: Bowker, 1978. 4 vols.

*International Who's Who*. London: Europa Publications, 1935– . Annual.

*Who's Who*. London: Black, 1849– . Annual.

*Who's Who in America*. Chicago: Marquis, 1899– . Biennial.

*Who's Who in the World*. Chicago: Marquis, 1970– . Biennial.

4. Reviews

*American Reference Books Annual*. Edited by Bohdan S. Wynar. Littleton, CO: Libraries Unlimited, 1970– . Annual.

*Book Review Digest*. New York: H.W. Wilson, 1905– . Monthly, except February and July, with annual cumulations.

*Book Review Index*. Detroit: Gale Research, 1965– . Bimonthly with annual cumulations.

*Choice*. Chicago: Association of College and Research Libraries, American Library Association, 1964– . Monthly except bimonthly July-August; annual index.

*An Index to Book Reviews in the Humanities*. Williamston, MI: Phillip Thomson, 1960– . Annual.

*Library Journal*. New York: Bowker, 1876– . Semimonthly except monthly July-August; annual index.

*New York Times Book Review Index, 1896– 1970*. New York: Arno, 1973. 5 vols.

5. Library Research Guides; Style Manuals

Aldrich, Ella V. *Using Books and Libraries*. 5th ed. Englewood Cliffs, NJ: Prentice-Hall, 1967. 147 pp.

Barzun, Jacques, and Graff, Henry F. *The Modern Researcher*. 3d ed. New York: Harcourt Brace Jovanovich, 1977. 378 pp.

*Cook, Margaret G. *The New Library Key*. 3d ed. New York: H.W. Wilson, 1975. 264 pp.

Gates, Jean Key. *Guide to the Use of Books and Libraries*. 4th ed. New York: McGraw-Hill, 1979. 292 pp.

*MLA Handbook for Writers of Research Papers, Theses, and Dissertations*. New York: Modern Language Association, 1977. 163 pp.

*The MLA Style Sheet*. 2d ed. New York: Modern Language Association, 1970. 48 pp.

*A Manual of Style for Authors, Editors, and Copywriters*. 12th ed., rev. Chicago: University of Chicago Press, 1969. 546 pp.

Strunk, William, Jr., and White, E.B. *The Elements of Style*. 2d ed. New York: Macmillan, 1972. 78 pp.

*Turabian, Kate L. *A Manual for Writers of Term Papers, Theses, and Dissertations*. 4th ed. Chicago: University of Chicago Press, 1973. 216 pp.

# Index of Titles

# Notes

# Notes

# Notes